SIGNIFICANT LIVES!

By: Jim Golden

Significant Lives! is a book born out of years of struggle and frustration as a Christian and a leader in the Charismatic Church. It is a book that will make you laugh and cry. It may just encourage you, too. It is a book that helps us remember that no matter what the circumstances look like — GOD, not man, is still in control.

ADDITIONAL AVAILABL BOOKS BY JIM (Also available in e-book format).

What is the GOSPEL of the Kingdom?

Counterfeit Christianity vs. the Kingdom of GOD!

PROPHECY—Search for the TRUTH!

SIGNIFICANT LIVES!

ISBN 978-0-557-18188-9

TABLE of CONTENTS

Introduction

By William Kellers

Most books that include personal illustrations need an objective introduction to provide a bridge between the reader and an unknown author. There are just some things that need to be said about Jim and are better said by someone other than himself. I read the original manuscript primarily because my friend wrote it, though I realize now that the message of the book pinpointed a need in my own life. Then Jim asked me to edit for him. I was honored by the request and it is my privilege to introduce the book-and him-to you.

My friendship with Jim and Terry gives me an "insider" advantage in understanding what God is saying through Jim's words. It is easy to expect an autobiography in the pages that lay ahead of you, but that expectation would blur the real message and purpose. Whether we're reading events from Jim's life or a parable in the Bible, it's easy to think we understand the simple story and yet miss the deeper revelation.

To avoid doing that, there are two important things to keep in mind as you read this book.

Introduction

First, its message was formed IN Jim's life THROUGH events soverignly ordained and initiated by God. In a very real sense Jim-his life, unique mannerisms, and style-IS the message.

Secondly, we must remember that God called Jim to function as a prophet, one who speaks FOR God. Though in this book he is both the message and the messenger, Jim draws attention-not to himself-but to the Person who sent the message.

Jim is only a voice speaking from a burning bush. But when a voice speaking from a burning bush gets our attention, we must respond to the message and to the One speaking through the fire. To hear and understand the revelation in these pages, prayerfully listen with the inner ear of your heart. We almost need to disregard the voice and the phenomenon used to speak the words. That means there is work for us to do as we read. Like gold miners, we must pan the words Jim wrote and separate the events of his life from the valuable ore that can enrich our own. You will find nuggets of truth. You'll experience their full value only after the rough ore is refined by the fiery trials in your life. You too will burn with devotion to Jesus and yet not be consumed.

You might ask, "Why should I read a book written by someone who is neither the successful pastor of a large church, nor the charismatic head of an international ministry?" As you read, remind yourself that God used public figures-kings and priests -to lead His people, build His house, and wage war. The record of what God did through those prominent figures became inspired scripture. But when God spoke to his people, He did so through prophets. Prophets often just appear on the scene, deliver their message, and vanish. Be aware! They may represent a little blip on the radar screen of history, but if you reject or miss the blip, you miss hearing God speak.

Since Jim's message comes from a private life with his Lord, it is easy to dismiss its public value. Yet it is that very fact-it happened privately, in obscurity-that makes it MORE valuable. The church needs popular pastoral books written by prominent leaders instructing people in the basics of Christian living. This is a prophetic book and may never be popular. Yet it is also needed because it was formed outside the main channels of Christian streams. It speaks a word into-not out of-the flow of Christian history.

Introduction

Most disciples of Jesus Christ remain so busy with life that they rarely see beyond surface issues. We are too much like a deer suddenly blinded and frozen in the lights of an oncoming car. Our focus is often fixed on the things in Christianity that shine the brightest, move the fastest, and ring the loudest. That's because the kingdom of this world has infiltrated Christianity. That unholy alliance produced a Christian world that produces worldly Christians. It lures people into busy, fast-paced, and flashy lifestyles that expect and demand quick outward success. *In trying to make optimum use of our time in this life, we inadequately prepare for the next.* Those who live an automated push-button Christianity will be hit by the oncoming car. A frozen focus on the brightest light will cause us to miss knowing the ONE who is THE Light.

In contrast, life lived in harmony with the kingdom of God moves slowly. God the Father, who is "The Ancient of Days" and who knows the end from the beginning, is never in a hurry. More than a surface relationship with Jesus Christ takes time to develop. God often hides His most precious saints in obscurity. Probably some of those reading this are also hidden. Thousands of believers in prisons around the world come to mind. Watchman Nee, after a fruitful public ministry in China, spent his last twenty years in a communist prison. Even in the western world, God has allowed the prison of circumstances to obscure the lives of many. He will allow any and all circumstances necessary to cause us to fix the eyes of our heart on Him.

We may be tempted to ask why God hides those who seem to most deeply love Him. We may justify a long season of obscurity as preparation for public ministry; but there again, our focus is on the outward results. God does it for His own sovereign reasons and that should be adequate. Before we ask "why," we need to remind ourselves of God's priorities. What does He love the most? This book focuses beyond DOING things that please Our heavenly Father. It urges us to BE one who loves the Lord Jesus Christ Himself. And isn't that what any prophet is primarily called to do?

Since the prophets often came out of wilderness obscurity, they usually weren't fashionably dressed in the styles of the day. Their message and style of delivery didn't win popularity contests. Though Jim is a good writer, frankly, his style is not "reader friendly." As I've said, you need to work and dig to get the gold from this book. If you'd prefer a light testimonial that tickles your ear, this is probably not for you. You may be satisfied with the status quo of Christian reading and that's all right. And if you're going to compare this literary format to best sellers, you can save your time. Yet, because you picked up a book that is not intended to be popular, you're probably prepared to pray through Jim's words to hear God speak. Do you want to read something that is anointed even if you have to go out in the wilderness to find it? This will not disappoint you.

Lastly, one other question may form in your mind as you read. You might wonder why God seems to speak so clearly and often to Jim. Does he have a hotline to heaven? When he says that God initiates and engages him in conversations-or gives him visions-does it mean that Jim is more gifted, special, or holy than the rest of us? **No!** You are also special to God. He gives gifts to His servants so that they can do what He called them to do and that means we all don't receive all the gifts. Though it seems like God is frequently speaking to Jim, in reality there are often weeks, months or years between revelations. Some of the chapters represent convictions that took years to form.

Collecting highlights of his times with God in a book distorts the fact that Jim lives an ordinary life. Again, focus should not be on the messenger but on the message and the sender. God speaks to Jim as he experiences the ordinary events of life-traveling a freeway, working a job, or playing with his children. God chooses the time and place. I suspect that He does the same with us all but possibly in a subtler manner. That's why Jim's message is suitable. He's a man who knows the common daily struggles and where you're at in them. He's been there too.

Jim writes what he receives in heavenly conversation. If God speaks and reveals while you read, you also receive the revelation He gave Jim. Not only that, but that revelation enhances your ministry gift. The challenge is that Jim is not only communicating information, but also revealing THE Person of Jesus Christ. He's like a counselor preparing an engaged couple for marriage. He can talk about marital intimacy but the couple must ultimately experience it for themselves. And so it is with you, this book, and your intimacy with Jesus. What happens in your private moments with your Lord is hidden and inaccessible from the eyes and influence of all. We can repeat God's own promise to meet with those who draw near to Him.

With that in mind, we extend the following blessing from 2 Peter 1 to all readers who have ears to hear: v.2..."Grace and peace be yours in abundance through the knowledge of God and of Jesus our Lord. ...v.8 For if you posses these qualities in increasing measure they will keep you from being ineffective and unfruitful in your knowledge of our Lord Jesus Christ.

PREFACE

The Vision:

"...They follow the Lamb wherever he goes..."Revelation 14: 4b NIV

In 1992, I was privileged to be part of a prayer group with men and women from all walks of life. Some were even in "full-time" ministry. Many different backgrounds and denominational upbringings were represented there.

Yet all these lovely people had one important thing in common. Their deep, almost insatiable hunger for the precious Lamb of God. These men and woman were willing to forsake all to follow the Lamb. When I speak of forsaking all, I am speaking of not only the bad things but the "good" things as well. Paul put it this way. "But what things were gain to me, those I counted loss for Christ." During one of our meetings I had a vision.

In my vision I saw a mountain that was high and very much like a tower. The pinnacle was shielded from view, but I instinctively knew that the throne of

God was there. Roads that encircled it, cutting into the mountain from its massive base to its narrowing pinnacle, divided this mountain. At first glance, it appeared that there was only one road spiraling up to the top. Upon closer inspection, I could see that there were many individual roads, like bands encircling the great mountain. As I searched for the secret of how to reach the top, suddenly I saw a nearly overgrown stairway that led straight up the face of the mountain linking all the individual roads together. The individual roads boasted signs like tradition, intercessory prayer, evangelism, and the restoration of the kingdom of God. However, at every crossroads where one of these roads intersected the stairway, there was also a sign pointing to the stairway that led to the top. It read **DEVOTION TO THE LAMB.**

Then I heard a voice speaking that was gentle yet so piercing that it went through me like a sword, and I began to weep. The voice told me that from time to time I had found the stairway that led straight to the throne of God. However, because of what seemed to be a severe ascent I would often get off onto one of the roads and walk around the mountain. I needed to learn what Paul meant when he said, "I press toward the mark for the prize of the high calling of God in Christ Jesus."

These roads seemed like good endeavors yet, they always led away from the stairway. At this point in my life, I was on one of the roads called intercessory prayer. Although it was closer to the top of the mountain than roads I had previously taken, I still had "the cart before the horse". The odds may favor the prayer warrior knowing Jesus intimately and being devoted to him, but it is still possible to miss the mark. As the voice called from the top of the mountain, I felt my heart being drawn. It said repeatedly, "Come Up Here!" Until I heard the voice, I was not aware of how lost or hungry and thirsty I had become. As I got closer to the stairway, a renewed sense of purpose and destiny gripped me. I felt like someone recovering from amnesia. Suddenly I remembered the reason I was alive. Suddenly I remembered my "betrothal to Jesus".

As I started back up the stairway the sense of extreme well-being invaded me. I noticed that on the face of each step something was written. I could not see what was written on the steps others were standing on, but I saw light begin to flow up through the tread of the step into the soles of their feet until it illuminated their entire body. As my foot touched each step I realized an area of great need in my life was being met. The Lamb is in the "business" of restoring our souls. To me he has been a friend to the friendless, a Father to the fatherless, the Lover of the unlovely and the One who accepts me unconditionally.

When I shared this with the group, an attitude of urgency enshrouded us. We saw how subtle and easy it is to leave the path of pure and simple devotion to God. Almost with one voice, we sought forgiveness and repentance. Then the others began to feel the same sense of unimaginable well-being I had experienced. We instinctively knew that none of these roads was bad. Jesus himself walked them all. The difference between his disciples, and us was that they walked the roads following the Lamb.

"They follow the Lamb wherever he goes" is speaking about the 144,000 mentioned in Revelation chapter 14, but I do not believe it is limited to them alone. Every "thing" we do must spring out of our devotion to Christ. If we are not living in a state of devotion to Him, it is the same as forsaking him. **"God has said, Never will I leave you, Never will I forsake you."** (Hebrews 13: 5 NIV) His devotion to us is steadfast and unshakable. It is always our level of devotion to him that must be questioned. Our whole life, as Christians, is to be a life of devotion to Jesus Christ. It's time we get back on the stairway and off the roads until the Lord takes us by the hand and says come follow me!

The Burden:

The Book **SIGNIFICANT LIVES** has been years in the writing. It has been renamed about five times and reflects a period of two decades of my

Christian life. My friend Bill Kellers who has watched its evolution from adolescence to adulthood, challenged me many times to say what I meant and to reveal what I felt as I lived out those years learning to shed the extra baggage most of Christendom seeks to place on its followers. This is not easily done. I watched my life go through two major transitions during this period. It started when I was twenty-three and had an encounter with Jesus Christ that changed my life forever.

I had been an "outlaw" biker and proud of it, boasting many times about the cruel and self-indulgent existence I had adopted. I gained everything in life I thought would bring me happiness but found myself deeply depressed. Sex, drugs and rock 'n' roll were the variety that spiced my life. As the old country song proclaimed, I too wanted to, *live fast, love hard, die young, and leave a beautiful memory.*

God's timing is impeccable. All my old friends are either dead or serving life sentences in prison. Jesus set me free just in time, and that is a very important point. If anyone could boast of knowing about slavery, it was me. I had lived a life of slavery that was destined to end tragically. The night I surrendered my life to Jesus and cried out for his help, he set me free from all my addictions, both mental and physical. The next day I had no withdrawal symptoms and had lost all desire for drugs. More than that, he made me feel like I was actually worth something. With Jesus, I never had to prove my worth. He always let me know the price that was paid to redeem me was great. For the first time in my life, I no longer felt alone.

What took place over the next twenty years is a difficult story to tell. I watched almost bewildered as the joy Christ gave me turned into sorrow. This book seeks to address the subtle yet heinous way men and women, can be ensnared and enslaved by a religious system that is not truly representative of Christ or true Christianity. It is written to you who are searching for, or have known the freedom that Jesus brings and have slowly seen organized religion drain that life and freedom away. This book is written for you who have been misused and abused through all the subtle innuendoes of everyday Christian conformity. You are fed up with Christianity and do not want to go to Church anymore. Alternatively, you are still going and if you were not afraid of what people would say, you would run through the doors shedding all the extra baggage as you ran.

Sometimes it is necessary to flee from the tyranny of *religion*. Christianity has become a religion just like all the other religions of the world. It was never meant to be so. It was always intended to be a relationship between each individual person and their Savior. Out of that vital relationship, a fellowship would be formed in the Spirit of his life and love. What stands today is not a monument to Jesus' sacrifice and love, but a demonstration of man's inability to duplicate the salvation of God through his own meager efforts. If you feel like a burnt offering and must flee-do not flee into the wilderness of doubt and despair, but into the loving arms of your only Savior-Jesus Christ.

Organized religion puts so much emphasis on appearances, but Jesus told Nicodemus that the Kingdom was invisible to all but those who were part of it. Religion's job is not to try to make a better Church, as if the work of Christ were somehow lacking, but to espouse Christ's followers to Christ. Because of its failure to do so, the word religion, as it is used in this volume, does not carry the favorable definition it does in most of society. Instead, it represents the lifeless structure created through man's feeble attempt to play God. Few of us ever come to know what it really means to trust Jesus with our lives. If we did, we would not constantly be trying to change each other.

This book is about a man who did not heed the warning of scripture and is still feeling the effects. The man is me, and I entrusted much of my life to men rather than Jesus alone. I was a slave set free by the sacrifice of Christ and then imprisoned by the vain philosophies of men. My desire for recognition coupled with the "carrot" of doing something great for God led me on like a donkey. What can we do for God that he has not already done for us? In addition, what greater work of God is there than pure and simple devotion to his Son Jesus Christ? Our loyalty to Jesus, not our loyalty to men, and their causes pleases God.

SIGNIFICANT LIVES is the result of the pain that we all experience simply by living in a less-than-perfect world. Its continual challenge is for the reader to allow the truth of God's word to reveal who God is and what we are because of his work of salvation, instead of the circumstances and situations of life-fight the good fight of faith. I kept the Chapters short deliberately, in order to foster meditation. I know what it is like to come home tired from work that the last thing you want to do is read another book on our responsibilities as good

Christians. It is my hope that this book will simply reveal all that God has already done and help you to respond to his ability. I do not want to turn you into people of responsibility but people with *respondability*.

It is for freedom that Christ has set us free. Stand firm, then, and do not let yourselves be burdened again by a yoke of slavery. Mark my words! I, Paul, tell you that if you let yourselves be circumcised, Christ will be of no value to you at all.

See to it that no one takes you captive through hollow and deceptive philosophy, which depends on human tradition and the basic principles of this world rather than on Christ.

CHAPTER ONE

Significant Lives

June 21, 1995 was my 23rd spiritual birthday, unless you count the trip down the aisle in 1957, when a "turn-or-burn" Baptist preacher scared me to the altar. July 2nd was my natural birthday. You notice I left out the particulars concerning this event. Let's just say I am older than 60. In the last number of years something has begun to happen to me that I never thought possible. I have become concerned about the over-all productivity of my life. Personally believing that the return of our Lord is imminent and looking at the "big-picture" of my life's accomplishments, I had begun to become discouraged. Did I say discouraged, it was probably more like depressed?

I thought by this time a man should be approaching the end of a career and planning for his retirement. However, I had just begun a new home business as a Christian Internet Provider (1994). I have not done this because of boredom with all my previous successes, but because, as a species we have a need to eat. My nickname is the *dancing bear*, and some have assured me that if I were to limit my physical activity I could possibly survive for a year without solid food. My wife and four children, however, are another story. They have become accustomed to their daily bread.

While food and eating is a favorite subject with me, I want to get back to a *greater need* that seems to beat within the breast of the western male and female of our species. I am referring to the need to be, or at least feel, productive. I believe it stems from a God-given need for significance. We all want to know that our lives have counted for something, are significant! As westernized Christians, we have translated the fulfillment of this need for significance into activity. Activity and productivity become synonymous in the mind of the western Christian. Even if we are not in "full-time" ministry most of us believe, that we are all God's ministers (ambassadors). While this is true, I want to suggest that how we should walk this out has been filtered through the gossamer web of 21st century western interpretation.

Not long ago I ministered as the Spirit was poured out on the church I attend. During this time I saw thousands become so weak they could no longer stand (commonly referred to as "slain" in the Spirit). God healed one blind man when I anointed his eyelids with oil, and a crippled woman stood and walked around the sanctuary holding my hand. Yet, because we have a tendency to focus on the activity of the Spirit, as my mother use to say, we cannot see **the tree** for the forest. Associating the activity of the God's Spirit with significance or productivity, we seldom realize this significant activity is the result of who He is. *All activity becomes memory and memories* *are poor substitutes for a growing and ongoing relationship with God's Spirit.*

Who else can heal the blind but God? Who else can make the cripple to walk and the deaf to hear? If your answer is other than, "no one but God," you are on shaky ground. It is a simple thing for God to do these things because he is light and in him there is no darkness at all. I am an electrician by trade so I know that when you walk into a dark room and flip on the switch, if you have electricity and a good light bulb, the darkness is going to disappear. It should follow that when *God comes on the scene,* as his child, if you have faith and need, darkness is going to disappear.

When someone is healed, it is not so much God doing something, as it is God being something. He is a creator and by virtue of being a creator, whenever he is present something is created. I am not speaking of God's universal presence but his manifested presence, which is open and available to all of his children. In fact, his *manifested presence* is what salvation is all about. All who have entered into Jesus' *salvation* will eventually see the veil that separated us from him torn in two from the top to the bottom. This veil, while representative of the veil that protected the priests from the manifested glory of God in the temple, not only exists in the temple of our hearts, but is just as effective in shielding us from God's life-giving glory. When Jesus died at Calvary this veil was torn in two down in the temple in the city. When God sends the Spirit of his son into our hearts, he begins a negotiation process with each of us to tear our veil in two. This can be a frightening idea. It struck terror into the hearts of many high priests. A rope was tied around their ankle in order to extricate the dead body of a high priest whose sacrifice was found unacceptable by God. We may be assured that if Jesus is our sacrifice God will find him acceptable.

This morning as I was reading John 14 I began to realize once again, that the place Jesus was going to prepare for us in his Father's house was not a little shack in the corner of glory-land. It was not going to be entered as the result of some future advent. Our translation into heaven, or Christ's physical return to earth would not bring us into this place, but his Father keeping his promise, and pouring out the Holy Spirit would alone bring about the fulfillment. As Jesus spoke to Philip and the others, it was easy to see his concern for his children. He can end our lives as spiritual orphans when we realize that the Spirit comes to *be* with us. Through His fathering and nurturing, He brings about a wonderful metamorphosis in each one of His children. He redefines significance in our lives. We begin to realize that anyone who is in this type of intimate relationship with the Almighty is significant. Not only do we have God's ear but also we have his life.

Before God is ever God through you—you are significant. Before his presence in you ever gives sight to the blind or leads someone to the threshold of the Kingdom-you are significant. You are significant because the blood and salvation of Jesus Christ has made you a species of being that has never before lived on planet earth—until Jesus did what he did. The secret to his doing was his being. The secret to our doing is not any different. If we want a life marked by the "presence" of God, we must allow the Holy Spirit to transform us into heaven-beings. We must allow him to take us into *the place* Jesus has prepared for us in his Father's house. Until he has our full attention and devotion, we will continue to struggle with the doing. Until we realize that he has come for deep and intimate transforming union with us, our life's definition of significance will continue to be defined as doing instead of being.

As we move into the next decade, we see the world looking for a people who wield the power of the age to come. These people know they are born from above and have found their significance in who they are rather than what they do. These people dwell in the secret place Jesus prepared for them and will once again turn the world upside down or, better stated, right side up. The miraculous activity that will spring forth from them will not be able to be contained, denied or kept secret. The life-giving presence of their heavenly Father will simply be what he is in them. Wherever they go they will truly be the children of the Most High God. Let us all begin to cry out for the friendship of the Holy Spirit and not just His activity then our lives will truly become significantly productive!

CHAPTER TWO

Mary or Martha —
Who Are You?

"There is only one thing needful,"

To say that life in the 21st century, especially in America, is fast-paced and confusing is an understatement. People make millions each year teaching others how to prioritize their lives. With so many things in the world vying for our attention the last thing we need are over-zealous *prophets* and *teachers* adding to our confusion. Many Christians are drowning in a sea of complexity when even the most unlearned person should be able to understand and flourish through the Gospel's message. Let us look at what Jesus has to say about complexity.

> As Jesus and his disciples were on their way, he came to a village where a woman named Martha opened her home to him. She had a sister called Mary, who sat at the Lord's feet listening to what he said. But Martha was distracted by all the preparations that had to be made. She came to Him and asked, "Lord, don't you care that my

> sister has left me to do all the work by myself? Tell her to help me!" **"Martha, Martha,"** the Lord answered, **"you are worried and upset about so many things, but only one thing is needed. Mary has chosen what is better and it will not be taken away from her."** (Luke 10: 38-42)

Words that stick out in our Lord's response to Martha's accusation of Mary's lack of assistance, and what appeared to be Jesus' indifference at her plight are: **one, needful, chosen** and **taken.** The thing we must remember about the scripture is that it is the Holy Spirit's voice to God's people. Through the Word he is able to reveal **himself** and his **ways** to us. He can show us what is important to him through the different stories he desired recorded in its pages.

If we will commit ourselves to respond to *his guidance* through *his word* he will pour out *his grace* bringing revolutionary change in our lives. I say all that to make us realize that this is not just a cute little story about an overworked woman frustrated by her lazy sister sitting at the feet of a worship-seeking Messiah. It is poignant in its diagnosis of the ills of the Church and the cure for all the associated problems facing her and the world today.

The first thing to notice is that Jesus had entered into her village. Jesus will always come within reach of us. Next was her response to him being there. She invited him into her home. It is important to note that Mary and Martha were sisters. It was probably *their* home. I believe they are a cross section of Christianity today. As Christians, we have opened our homes to Jesus, haven't we? I tell my children that they must watch what they eat because their bodies are the temples of God. In this sense, all Christians open their *homes* to the Master when we ask him to be our Lord and Savior.

The next verse shows us the most important thing we can do once we open our *home* to Jesus: sit at his feet and listen to him! "But Martha was distracted with all the preparations that had to be made." In our Christian lives, many preparations must be made in order to accommodate the ministry of the Lord. The *key* is **NOT** allowing them to become an encumbrance or distraction. The only way I know how to do that is by allowing Jesus to do the preparatory work in us. Jesus is called the author and finisher of our faith. God is at work in us both to will and to work his good pleasure. He that has begun a good work in us will bring it to maturity. The capper of all is, *"... are you so foolish, having begun in the Spirit are you now made perfect by the flesh?"*

It is important to remember that none of these *things* or *preparations* can be done in our own strength. They must come about in the timing of the Lord or we run the risk of producing mere external change!

I am sure that Martha must have felt a little jealousy toward her sister. She also wanted a little recognition for all her service from Jesus, or she would have spoken to Mary privately about her *irresponsibility*. Martha had made the mistake that we all make at one time or another, the mistake of assumption. She assumed that the Lord wanted her to do all these things. Little did she expect the response she received.

Now don't get me wrong, Martha was very precious to the Lord. She just had her priorities a little out of order and it was affecting her life and the lives of those around her. I was taught that we should go to those in authority in a *spirit of inquiry* when we do not agree with something that is going on. Somehow, I do not think Martha quite had the right idea of what an inquiring attitude was. She starts out her sentence with the word **Lord,** but her question sounds more like an accusation than an inquiry. When she commands Jesus to tell her sister to help her it removes most of the doubt from my mind. The translators should have reversed the words *don't* and *you* to read, "Lord *you don't* care that my sister has left me to do all the work. Tell her to help me!" How many times we say the right things but inside we are just like Martha! The problem is Jesus can read between the lines. He hears just as clearly what we *don't* say as what we *do* say!

I believe that her conversation with Jesus is reflective of much of our prayer life as Christians. We go to the Lord and pour out our complaints. Yet seldom do we even wait for his response. It is evident that she just wanted her feelings made known. She was not concerned whether her question was received as a question or accusation. For so long I thought Jesus said her name twice as a means of comforting her until I had children of my own. Many times when we speak to our children, we have to say their names twice to get their attention. I believe that is exactly what Jesus was doing with

Martha. If her question had truly been a question she would have been waiting for the answer. However, Jesus says, *"Martha, MARTHA, you are worried and upset about many things."* Immediately we know she is in trouble, if she heard his sermon on the mount, because he classifies worry as sin and unbelief.

He then goes on to imply that she has done nothing to serve him because she has not been sitting at his feet listening to his word. The scripture tells us to wait for the Lord. The eyes of the servant are on the hand of the Lord. We, like Jesus, must do only the things that the Father tells us to do. I wonder how long Jesus will have to say my name two or three times to get my attention. I wonder how much of our service is assumption? How often do we sit at his feet and simply do what he tells us to do? Jesus declared Mary's actions to be the only thing that was needful for us to do in the role of our preparation for him. He said that it was a choice that we have to make. Once we make this choice, he will not permit anything to endanger it.

Many times we find it much easier to keep busy than to be still in God's presence for fear of what he might say, or what we should say. Something that has brought me peace in this area is knowing that God has already written all my days in his book, before there ever was one. Honesty is the best policy. When I was his enemy, he gave his life on the cross for me. Knowing his love and acceptance prepares me to receive any word from him, no matter how hard. Knowing his wisdom and power creates faith in me. His word does not just expose my bankruptcy but, when acknowledged, fills my lack. He more than pays my debts and shortcomings with his immeasurable grace.

Like never before there is a need for revival being recognized among God's people. Like never before, we must learn to sit at his feet and listen to his voice. Jesus said that his words were *spirit* and *life*. Job said that he treasured the words of God's mouth more than his daily bread. Jesus said that man didn't live by bread alone but by every word that came from the mouth of God. It is no wonder that the devil would like to turn us into a *performance-based society* rather than *the Society of Jesus*. Satan knows that if he can keep us distracted with what appears to be the *good* preparations for the Lord he can keep us from hearing the words of eternal life and of truly becoming his servants.

Unless we give up our agendas, we will never receive his agenda. The attitude that was in Mary's heart needs to grip and consume the heart of the Church today. I pray that we all learn what it means to be *God's servant* and not just *a servant*. The confidence and results that come from speaking for God will once again turn the world upside down. It is time to sound the trumpet, take the keys to the Kingdom, and unlock the power of the age to come.

> The call to war is going forth to every man woman and child of God. It is time to put on God's armor and change the face of this planet in the power of His might. God does not need any

special gifts or great natural abilities. He only requires your devotion and availability. If you will listen closely, you might just hear his still small voice saying, "Whom shall I send?" I pray your answer will be, *"Here I am Lord, send me!"* If we do not learn to be his friend, and abide in him, we may have to pass the torch on to another generation. If we do, I pray that it is a torch that burns brightly with our sincere love and devotion for Jesus Christ!

CHAPTER THREE

Who Has Bewitched You?

You foolish Galatians! Who has bewitched you? Before your very eyes Jesus Christ was clearly portrayed as crucified. I would like to learn just one thing from you: Did you receive the Spirit by observing the law, or by believing what you heard? Are you so foolish? After beginning with the Spirit, are you now trying to attain your goal by human effort? Have you suffered so much for nothing-if it really was for nothing? Does God give you his Spirit and work miracles among you because you observe the law, or because you believe what you heard?

I sat on my back porch playing my guitar with tears in my eyes. As I sat there, I was pondering the last two decades of my life as a Christian. The end of this road now found me in debt, out of work for the 14th time in seven years, and feeling like a real failure. Being out of work and in debt were not the reasons. In today's economy that is not unusual. What was causing my sense of failure was my inability to find my place of service for God and those special relationships we all dream of as Christians. Echoing repeatedly in the background of my thoughts came the phrase, *"Who has bewitched you?"* Most of us should ask this question ourselves today.

Before I was born, my biological father told my mother she would have a son who would be born with white hair. He would grow up and become a preacher. This was before she knew she was pregnant. This man never married my mother, why, I never found out. It was a question I avoided. I thought not knowing was better than actually hearing that he rejected me. Now that my mother has passed away I may never know. However, that prophecy, as it were, along with all the other confirming words from esteemed men of God only added to my sense of failure. Not only was I out of work but try as I would the ability to come, or get into some meaningful service for God was constantly eluding me.

Then my thoughts began to wander back down the road I had walked. When I was first *born again* and filled with the Holy Spirit, life was much different. I walked with God in simplicity. Miracles were expected occurrences. I simply heard the voice of my new heavenly father and did what he told me. As a result, blind eyes were opened, a dead man was raised back to life and many other wonderful things took place. My joy was overflowing.

Suddenly the thought came to me that I had more harm done to me as a Christian than I had done to me as an unbeliever. *"Who has bewitched you,"* the still small inner voice said to me again. *"You were doing so well, running the race."* I began to feel tears run down my cheek, but without the normal feelings that usually accompany crying, as though pain was surfacing that was so deep within me my mind wasn't fully aware it was there.

I thought back to my first experiences in working with a group of men in building the Kingdom of God. How they sought to *harness* the potential power of God within me. They undertook my discipleship and ordained me as a pastor. When it was all over I was left much worse off than when we had met. It was partially my fault. I allowed myself to be seduced by the enticing words of men's wisdom and the promise of glory. I had put my hope in man rather than God and my heart contracted a disease called *deferred hope*. For all practical purposes, I had been bewitched!

I could hear Paul's piercing words ringing in my ears, *Are you so foolish? After beginning with the Spirit, are you now trying to attain your goal by human effort?* God had begun his fathering of me. He wanted to teach me his ways but like most children who get old enough to think they know something I mistakenly turned to someone else for my guidance. The stage was well set for this desertion. Subconscious fear of being led astray caused me to put my trust in man instead of God. Verses like, *"In the multitude of counsel there is safety."* were skillfully used to persuade me into disregarding other scriptures like, *"But when he, the Spirit of truth, comes, he will guide you into all truth."* Slowly over a period of 10 years, I watched as the joy of my salvation and the power of God drained out of me.

17

The problem with putting your hope in man is the dependency that comes along for the ride. Eventually, even the most saintly of men will abandon you. When this happens we are left feeling inadequate to move on in the life of the Spirit. The only one we can ever really be dependent on and not disappointed by is Jesus. As Adam fell in the garden, when he chose to be independent, so I had chosen to be dependent on someone other than God and fell. This is a shared transgression. Just like Adam was seduced into becoming independent so we are being seduced into putting our trust in men. Men may sometimes make good companions but they always make poor gods. All of our instructions as leaders should turn the eyes and the hearts of God's children to God.

I am beginning to experience a small portion of what I knew when I first walked with Jesus in simplicity. My prayer is that I have not suffered in vain. If you are reading this and are in a similar boat or moving in the same direction, I was, heed my words. The Lord is faithful and able to keep whatever is committed to his care. He is a faithful Father and a jealous God. He not only desires but also demands the right to raise and nurture his children. Do not let fear of any kind enter in between you and your loving Savior. Heed my words and I will not have suffered in vain.

It may be true that more damage can be done to us at the hands of *well meaning* Christians, than at the hands of the *ungodly.* God is the Ancient of Days, the Wonderful Counselor, the Mighty God, and the Everlasting Father. Why would we entrust our souls to anyone else? I am concerned over those who have said that they will give an account for my soul by becoming my teachers. No matter how well meant their intentions were the end-product of usurping God's role in someone's life is misuse and abuse. I want to go on record as forgiving them and releasing them from their sin to me in this area, as I ask forgiveness of those I have abused in a like manner.

In our youthful zeal we often usurp God's role in the lives of those we touch. In the things of God, the oldest among us is still an infant. Before it is too late let us all clothe ourselves with the garments of humility and repentance and return to our Heavenly Father's faithful arms today.

CHAPTER FOUR

That You Might Know Him

It was still very gray outside as I saw the first prospects of the rising sun begin to add substance and form to the shadows of my unfinished bathroom. It had become a place of solitude lately. It used to boast a 5-foot California Redwood hot tub in its more prosperous days, but recently hard times had forced it to sacrifice itself on the auction block for the welfare of the family. Did I say recently? That was in 1987. I can remember when it seemed like a month between weekends and now it seems like a month between years. One funny thing about aging is, time becomes a very precious commodity. That is as it should be.

In February of 1994 an old friend of mine prophesied to me concerning some things that God wanted to do in my life. One of them was to teach me some things about meditation, meditation on the person of God. I have long been a fan of A.W. Tozer's writings, especially his small but powerful volume called **THE KNOWLEDGE OF THE HOLY**. In his book he speaks of the attributes of God as things an unknowable God has revealed about himself that are true, so that we finite creatures might worship our infinite Creator.

For many years, it had been a volume that I would return to time after time. More recently, it had become a means by which God was beginning to fulfill my friend's prophecy.

I had just finished reading the chapter on the faithfulness of God and began to meditate on the implications of God's faithfulness, when His Spirit seemed to flood the room with wisdom and revelation. I began to see all the times I had been engaged in the practice of what I call subconscious, unworthy meditation of him. Simultaneously, he was revealing the truth concerning his faithfulness to me. Yes, what usually happens in a situation like this happened, I began to weep. Seeing the immutable faithfulness and love of God for me, through the eyes of the Spirit, made my highest and most noble thoughts of him teeter on the edge of insult and blasphemy.

As the Spirit of God began to give flight to my earth-bound mind I began to move from the realm of "creature-words and thoughts" into the realm of "spiritual knowledge." I feel somewhat like Paul, who struggled for the words to express what the Spirit revealed to him about God on his journey into the third heaven. He finally was satisfied to say that he saw and heard things which were unlawful and unutterable. The NIV translation puts it this way, *"I know a man in Christ who fourteen years ago was caught up to the third heaven. Whether it was in the body or out of the body I do not know- God knows. And I know that this man-whether in the body or apart from the body I do not know, but God knows-was caught up to paradise. He heard inexpressible things, things that man is not permitted to tell."* (2 Cor. 12:2-4).

I believe he was not permitted to speak about these things for two possible reasons. The first reason is that the revelation of who God is cannot be expressed in the mere words of men. God is so unlike anything that we can perceive that our most noble thoughts cannot even exist in the same galaxy with the reality of God. When the Prophets and Apostles spoke, of his heavenly glory they only had comparative terms to help their readers or listeners imagine what they saw. They would say things like, "He was like unto...or...he lives in unapproachable light..." I, however, am not trying to describe the physical appearance of God but the incredible nature of God. And I find myself harnessed by the same restraints as those who have gone before me. There are no words, thoughts, or meditations that can even begin to do our God justice. The second reason is, God wants us all to have this intimate knowledge of him on a first-hand basis.

As I said earlier, seeing the immutable faithfulness and love of God for me made my highest and most noble thoughts of him teeter on the edge of insult and blasphemy. Even though this is a comparative statement, what must ignoble and depraved thoughts be like? I am certain that everyone who names the name of Jesus is worthy of death a thousand times over for blasphemy if it is looked at in this light. How many times have we allowed the circumstances and situations of life that didn't go just the way we thought they should, to become the accuser of our God?

Blasphemy and idolatry are strange "bed-fellows" frequenting the normal Christian's life all too often. The reason we do not recognize them is because of our life's focus. Our eyes are usually turned inward. To us, sin is the nasty and unloving little things we do. Most of us do not even consider the sin of our thought life. Yet every Sunday, most of us try to worship a God that we have hardly thought of throughout the week, and if we have, our thoughts certainly were not worthy of him. Yet God who is rich in mercy has asked us to worship him, and to worship him in spirit and truth. I have come to believe that apart from the presence and anointing of his Holy Spirit it is impossible to accomplish this. Worship is an intimate communication, so tender and personal between God and his child, as to be compared with the relationship existing between a man and a woman in the act of consecrating the wedding bed.

As I began to cry out for the Spirit of wisdom and revelation in the *knowledge* of God, fear and deep reverence came upon me. I was afraid to offend the Holy One who had become the lover of my soul. I quietly, almost secretly sought for words to speak in appreciation, but found my tongue and mind almost terror-stricken by the possibility of insulting him. Yet He graciously and lovingly receives every feeble attempt at worship. Then I began to realize why Paul said that he spoke in tongues more than everyone else, and why the hymnist cried out for a thousand tongues to sing his Great Creator's praise.

Revival is beginning to sweep our country and reports are coming in from other parts of the world as well. The devil would most certainly like to misdirect our focus to the accompanying phenomena, rather than the fruitful reunion of intimate communion with our Father. I pray that not all the wonderful things that are taking place because of the outpouring of his Spirit become the center of our focus. In our Father, being, doing, thought, and expression, are the same. However, we are not ones such as him. We always seem to be about the doing part without the being part. If we would see this move of God's precious, manifested presence preserved, then all activity or ministry must come out of relationship. *"Now this is eternal life: that they may know you, the only true God, and Jesus Christ, whom you have sent."* John 17:3 (NIV). I want to encourage everyone reading this to fall into agreement with Jesus and allow the blessed third person of the Trinity to take you into the place where the Seraphim cry, "Holy, Holy, Holy," day and night. In that place, you will be changed forever.

CHAPTER FIVE

On A Hill Far Away

The Cross is the universal symbol of our Christian faith. We can see it fashioned in gold or silver and hanging around the necks of true Christians and unbelievers alike. It adorns ears and altars and may even be found in the cheeks and nostrils of some of our more *radical* children. It has been the inspiration of Christian hymnody throughout the ages. Yet for most of us the Cross is simply old and rugged and on a hill far away.

In Peter's day the cross was an insignia of terror and quite often lined the roads of the occupied nations of the Roman Empire. It was an ancient form of fatal torture improved upon by Rome and usually reserved for the most heinous offenders. Originally offenders were actually crucified to a tree. However, some ingenious fellow adapted the principle making it portable. Now one could be hung on a tree in a place where trees were rare and in any location the executioner deemed most effective.

Used successfully to quell rebellions, you would never see its likeness dangling from a chain around someone's neck. Women coming home from visiting a relative in a neighboring village would walk the cross lined roads in dread. Shielding their eyes from the nakedness of these grim reaper's victims, they would look at their faces silently praying that they would not recognize anyone.

Scripture even declared that death on a cross (or tree as it was often called-Duet. 21:23) was a sign of God's curse upon the one who died in such a manner. Is it any wonder that against such a backdrop Jesus might have been misunderstood? In his call for people to follow him, he spoke of the cross. Then he said to them all: *"If anyone would come after me, he must deny himself and take up his cross daily and follow me."* Luke 9:23 (NIV) My guess is that this particular sentence cut his following by at least 50%. Or many simply rationalized the literalness of his statement away.

God takes what is wretched, vial, and turns it into something beautiful and cherished. None of us has a problem embracing the symbolism of the cross but actually embracing it literally seems a near impossibility. Paul declared that he was crucified with Christ yet we all know that he was not actually one of the two men crucified with Jesus. To a 21st century believer, Paul's statement opens the door to some astounding possibilities.

I would like to follow a path of departure from the orthodox interpretations of this verse. Tradition interprets this as the surrendering of our will to God's will. But the cross is far more than simply a place of "death-to-self." The Cross is a place of revelation, creation and finality. Jesus said that a prerequisite to the cross was denying self. All through our lives, self is continually spewing forth the impressions of being alive. However, God says that we are totally separated from the giver of life. From the first breath we take only one thing is certain, we will take a last breath also. Self is a creature that stands on its own, quite unaware of its need for God.

At the cross we are forced to admit that we have no life within us-we are dead. At the cross, we are forced to bury our old dead spirit with its depraved human nature. At the cross God dissolves the chasm between us and reconciles us to Himself. He does this by literally removing our old heart of stone and putting into us a brand new heart. In this new heart of flesh, which is the seat of our nature, He weaves the thread of His own divine nature until only one fabric can be recognized. This weaving of His divine nature with the thread of our nature transforms our entire being as He renews our minds.

Understanding one basic principle is imperative to us who believe. Heaven does not deal in commodities. In heaven, the first order of business is a person. He is central and supreme. Everything begins and ends in Him. Jesus alone is the gross national product of heaven. Jesus alone is heaven's only export. The resurrection isn't a day it's heaven's champion. Revival is not a time or season it's the Lord strong and mighty, the Lord mighty in battle. When God speaks of writing his laws upon our hearts, He is actually speaking of His immutable choice to become one with His redeemed children.

From His vantage point on the cross, Jesus could see quite clearly. His plea for His Father to forgive us was a revelation in itself. Jesus said, *"Father, forgive them, for they do not know what they are doing."* Luke 23:34a (NIV). For such a long time I was content to accept orthodoxy's interpretation of this verse until I began to see through His eyes. Jesus came to die on the cross. He predetermined the method of his death. The people that would accomplish this had been released by God to do it. Granted they did not understand all the implications of crucifying God's Son but I do not believe Jesus was speaking merely of the act of crucifixion.

Jesus was gazing down on a race of beings he had created with his own hands for a much higher purpose. They were created to be the dwelling place of the great God Jehovah. A living temple that should have been in continual fellowship and harmony with God had turned into a blind and empty house of stone. However, from his vantage point on the cross he also knew that a new age was getting ready to dawn. He was becoming the progenitor of a new race. He was becoming the doorway into the awesome manifest presence of God. He was becoming the prototype of a new species of beings, fashioned in heaven by the will of God and breathed from the nostrils of the Almighty!

Everything about this new race from heaven would be pleasing to God. Soon all of creation would witness the birth of a people conceived in the mind of God before the beginning of time, a people truly for His own possession. They, like Jesus, would long to do the will of Him that sent them.

Created and born out of heaven they would only be passing through. Heaven was their home and down here, they would be ambassadors of another world. Their only mission would be a ministry of reconciliation. They, like Jesus, would go about doing *good* and healing all that were oppressed of the devil. They would literally turn the world *right side up*.

If you are like me you're probably wondering what went wrong. I feel that the Lord gave me the answer. In the first century, the devil was caught unaware. He did not know what happened. It took him awhile to recover and weave an appropriate web of deception. He had to come up with a plan that would give him access to the inaccessible community of heaven. The community of the redeemed could only be entered through the "old-man." The "old-man" or dead spirit was the product of Adam's decision to follow Satan in the garden. Jesus told the unregenerate Jews that their father was the devil (John 8:44). However, God had so thoroughly severed this relationship that only time and deception could give Satan place again.

Satan's chief weapon is deception. His modus-operandi was to imitate the old man. Speaking to these new children of God persistently in the first person, he eventually filled them with sufficient unbelief. They began to doubt themselves and God's salvation. Satan had found the landing strip he needed to launch his assault against the Bride of Christ. As God's children began to believe that Satan's thoughts and desires were their own, a veil began to form once again in the temple. Much of our theology today only adds layers to this veil increasing its opacity. Much of what we call speaking the truth in love is anything but the truth.

Let's take up the true cross of Calvary on which Jesus ended Adam's race. Each day, let us come to the place where Jesus birthed heaven's children. I urge you to begin to agree with the words and work of God daily. If anyone be in Christ he is a new creation. Whenever I meditate on God's salvation tears come to my eyes. The mouth of the Accuser of the Brethren is silenced and a voice within me begins to cry out, "I really do love God and want to serve Him."

The revelation that those vile lusts and evil desires might be coming from a source other than me releases the delivering hand of God in my life and sets me free from the power of the enemy. I want to declare to you that the new creation or child of God is just like Jesus. In addition, once we can silence the Accuser's voice we will actually begin to see ourselves as God sees us. Allow Jesus to wash your feet right now and ask Him to reveal more of His salvation to you.

And we, who with unveiled faces all reflect the Lord's glory, are being transformed into his likeness with ever-increasing glory, which comes from the Lord, who is the Spirit.

2 Cor. 3:18 (NIV).

Ask Jesus to destroy this veil of self-doubt and doubt in God's salvation and help us fix our eyes on Him once again. Don't leave the cross on a hill far away, make it a place you come to each day!

CHAPTER SIX

The Truth — What is it really?)

"So from now on we regard no one from a worldly point of view"

I used to think that "speaking the truth in love" was pointing out someone's faults and helping them set up a planned regimen to overcome them. While this could be part of the picture it's only a tiny part of the process, at best. The majority of the process we call, speaking the truth in love, should be proclaiming what God says in Scripture about us is true, *sometimes in the face of apparent contradiction.*

If the brand of truth you speak the most falls into the first category, make sure you have God's permission to speak this way to his children. Have you ever listened to someone telling one of your children what is right or wrong, or what to do? I do not know about you but that just, *"chafes my hide."* This is a very sensitive area with me and should not to be taken lightly when it comes to speaking to **God's** children. Permission and presumption both begin with the letter "P" but that is where the similarity must end. As a father part of my role is to lovingly correct, admonish and guide the development of my children. We must remember that it is no different for our heavenly Father. He is desirous of fulfilling this role with his spiritual children if we will clear the way. God knows that if he fulfills his role in fathering each of us our eyes will be fixed primarily on him and not each other.

He is the God of all encouragement, not discouragement. He has given us an everlasting righteousness equal to his own righteousness. In His eyes, his Son's sacrifice allows us stand beyond reproach forever. Jesus surely is not the Accuser of the Brethren. He knew every single wrong thing we would ever do before He died for us. Even with this knowledge, he accepted us unconditionally, and gave his life for us.

It is the Holy Spirit's "job" to convict the World of sin and of righteousness and of judgment. More often, we are told to simply love and accept. To encourage each other daily is not only a command but has a protecting power for the heart.

The salvation Christ sealed for us by shedding his blood is in effect eternally. *It is finished* and cannot be changed by mere mortals or any other power. Before we were born or had a chance to sin he had written our names in his Book of Life. Our confession and belief has assured they will never be "blotted" out. This knowledge gives each one of us the courage we need to face each day victoriously. We must remember that the victory that overcomes the world is our faith. Satan is the one who tries to drag us down and steal our courage.

I am devoting a lot of time to this subject for two reasons: First, because Jesus said it was the truth that would set us free. Secondly, because knowing the truth about ourselves will affect the way we treat others.

Paul told the Romans that believing with the heart and speaking with the mouth justified and saved us. It is therefore imperative that what we believe and speak line up with God's declaration of salvation. We know in our hearts that Jesus has justified us, but in the way, we deal with each other's faults and shortcomings we seldom declare the authority of his shed blood or finished work to each other as the solution. We seldom direct the needy one's gaze to their victorious Savior, Jesus Christ.

Paul proclaimed Christ and him crucified! How easy it is to overlook the obvious. Speaking the truth in love is literally speaking Jesus into someone's heart. Speaking the truth in love is clothing the nakedness of our brothers and sisters in the righteousness of Jesus, not further exposing their weakness or failure. Speaking about his ministry to us and his finished work causes us to fix their eyes on him. The gaze that is fixed on the beauty of Jesus soon loses interest in the things of this world and its attractions of the flesh. This is speaking truth in its purest form.

I don't want to leave the impression that any mere mortal, redeemed or not, has the ability to create anything with their words. God alone can do this. However, we may reveal his established truth with our words. The point I want to make is that in the multitude of "truths" being proclaimed today, there is only one truth that is THE TRUTH! *Today Christians are drowning in a sea of complexity.* Their loyal support and allegiance is being solicited by every teacher and movement in existence. Where are the men and women who will simply lead us to the living truth, **Jesus Christ**? Everything we say and do should flow from and return to the Lord Jesus Christ!

Eternity does not possess enough time to proclaim the Excellencies of God's glory yet; Sunday morning often finds the pulpits of our great nation hard-pressed to speak of this glory for only one hour. Is it because we cannot proclaim abundantly what we barely know superficially? ***"Out of the abundance of the heart the mouth speaks."***

I have noticed over the last 20 years a theology gain strength that centers mainly on what Paul called a *"worldly point of view"* or *"sight truth"* as I call it. This type of Christianity, I am convinced, brings no pleasure to God. On the contrary, it is displeasing as well as dishonoring to him. It entrenches its followers deep in pride and self-righteousness, and at the same time, causes them to believe they are actually doing God a service.

A closer inspection of 2 Corinthians might help us see that the "unseen" claims of God have set into motion a salvation that MUST reach perfection no matter what the *temporal* or *"seen"* proclaims. I suggest you take a moment to read chapters 3-5 so that they might be fresh in your thoughts.

We must understand Paul's call and apostolic mission to fully understand his writings. His orthodox life and subsequent conversion experience is the foundational platform on which God built Paul's mission and message to the world. He was raised as Saul, an orthodox Jew. His life and culture revolved around the Mosaic Law and its observance. Hundreds of precepts and interpretations had been added to the Mosaic Law that were tenaciously espoused and rigidly observed.

Paul's life was devoted to obeying these laws. His obedience to them was his basis for security and acceptance by God and his fellow Jews. The Law was meant to reveal the purity and holiness of God to his people, and eventually lead them to the Messiah. But the years distorted the Law so much that its precepts had taken the place of God and obscured Him from view.

On the road to Damascus Paul would meet his God for the first time and be blinded by his brilliance. During the ensuing weeks God would take this proponent of orthodoxy and systematically dismantle his theology through the revelation of the Holy Spirit. Paul would enter into a passionate and jealous love affair with the Son of God and grace would be the "tie that binds". This affair would cause him to be stripped of his notoriety and be considered deranged by his contemporaries. He would become an outcast to most of the Jews he proclaimed this Gospel of grace too. His life would often be in danger.

He would spend much of his time trying to preserve the simplicity of the Gospel from those who tried to add anything to its message of grace and hope in Christ. He would finally end up in prison and, as history records—beheaded for his witness. At the cost of his reputation and life he proclaimed the truth of the glorious Gospel of God's grace and love. This works-versus-grace war filled all of his writings. It didn't stop with his burial, but continues to this day.

This "foolishness" remained with Paul until the executioner's ax silenced him and he could proclaim the truth of grace no longer. Only when death took his voice did he cease to declare, *"For by grace are you saved through faith, and that not of yourself. It is the gift of God and not of works lest any man should boast."* This theme is the heart and soul of his theology and from this perspective all that he writes is better read.

Paul speaks of the glory of the new covenant, telling us that where the Spirit of the Lord is, there is freedom. Is what you are doing producing that sense of freedom? Do you have the freedom to fail without fear of what others might think, or to simply be whom and what you are without feeling ashamed or is failure fatal in your circle?

"If the Son shall make you free you shall be free indeed." His words are spirit and life. Speaking his truth in love is liberating, causing its hearers to enter his rest. You won't be worried about what others will think of you because you

know that you have been clothed in God's precious Son's life and he thinks of you very highly.

Paul says, *"...we do not lose heart. Rather, we renounce secret and shameful ways; we do not use deception, nor do we distort the word of God."* Remembering the place Paul is coming from we can begin to see what he really means. When it does not look like or feel like we are as saved as God claims, faith in Jesus is all the security we need, so don't lose heart.

Instead of trying to look good on the outside, we actually renounce this kind of shameful deception and speak openly of our weakness and failures. We do not try to distort the word of God to explain this apparent contradiction, or bring people into bondage by forcing them to adhere to anything or anyone but Jesus. It does not matter if unbelievers do not understand the light of the glorious Gospel of Christ. Even if peer pressure is so great it becomes violent in its desire for us to accept "outward" forms of change, because of the Spirit's life in us we cannot relent!

Paul says later in chapter 5 that what we are is plain to God and he hopes that it is plain to our conscience. You might be able to fool others and yourself. Even Hitler began to believe his own propaganda. However, we cannot fool God. He knows that as long as we live in these mortal bodies we are naked, and exposed to being corrupted by our mortal desires.

Just prior to Paul's meeting with Jesus on the road to Damascus, he would have considered himself to be *"as*

touching the righteousness which is of the law, blameless."
At the end of his life, from a worldly perspective, it would
appear that he got worse not better. Statements like, *"I thank
God, who sent Christ into the world to save sinners, of whom
I am chief,"* only served to affirm his degeneration in the sight
of his orthodox peers.

Paul also said when we beheld Jesus or reflected on his glory
with an "unveiled" face we were transformed. My
grandmother used to say that someone was "puttin' on airs" if
they were pretending to be something they weren't. Putting
on airs or putting a veil over our face has about the same
crippling effect.

Roy Hession, in the preface of his book, **WE WOULD SEE
JESUS** says, "Grace permits us to come (nay demands that we
come) as empty sinners to be blessed, empty of right feelings,
good character, and satisfactory record, with nothing to
commend ourselves but our deep need, fully and frankly
acknowledged. Then grace being what it is, is drawn by that
need to satisfy it, just as water is drawn to the depth that it
might fill it." "The struggle, of course, is to believe it and be
but empty sinners to the end of our days, that grace may
continue to match our needs."

If this can be considered as the truth then we must consider
most of the effort we spend in trying to make ourselves look
better as wasted effort. Because Paul knew that the one who
raised the Lord Jesus from the dead would also raise all
believers with Jesus and present them with him in God's

presence, he considered any effort that produced external change only a waste of time and a degradation of God's promise to perfect us.

Paul's confidence in the often "unseen" results of the finished work of Christ stemmed from what he referred to as the "deposit of the Spirit." He claimed it was God's guarantee of the change that was to come in our hearts, throughout this life, and finally to be completed upon the demise of our earthly temples. To the Angels in heaven and the Jewish mind it was an awesome, almost unbelievable, proposition for mankind to be the living temple of a Holy God. Only those deemed acceptable by God could live through such an experience without being consumed. No wonder Paul was convinced that God's salvation was complete, since his flesh was not devoured when God filled him with his Holy Spirit. *(Selah)*

As long as Paul lived, he struggled with the paradox of appearances vs. the finished work of Christ and the resulting war between works and faith as a means of justification. He tells us not to loose heart, even though outwardly we may appear to be wasting away, there is a glorious change-taking place on the inside. We must constantly proclaim this glorious truth to each other.

"So we fix our eyes NOT on what is seen, but on what is unseen. For what is seen is temporary, but what is unseen is eternal." He goes on to say how we long to be clothed with our heavenly dwelling so we will not be naked. For as long as we are alive in this body, we WILL be unclothed. In other

words, we will never fully "arrive" while on planet earth. But there is this longing to be "perfect" or more "pleasing" to God beating within our breast. How can we be more pleasing or perfect than Jesus? While the difference between uncreated God and his redeemed created beings is beyond measure, when God looks at us he sees us clothed with the life of his Son, Jesus!

It is this longing however; to eliminate these "perceived inconsistencies" coupled with our insecurities I believe the enemy capitalizes on. We are such creatures of sight and feeling that Satan plays on the "apparent" contradictions that exist in our lives. God says we are changed but we do not act that way, and if we do act that way we don't always feel that way. Satan then gets us to doubt the completeness of God's salvation through these inconsistency" in our lives. Because we love God and do not want people to think ill of him, because of our actions, we allow Satan to seduce us into trying harder to prove that, "God isn't a liar."

Alas, for many, speaking the truth in love has become a burdensome effort to transform ourselves into an acceptable image of salvation. We want to look good for the world and Christendom and think this will "please" God. Yet we bring each other into bondage and actually, "make Christ of no effect."

If we want to make it our goal to please him, then no matter whether we feel "close" to him or "away" we must live by faith and not by sight. To live, or be alive, is to experience God's uncreated life within us, transforming us from the inside out. Our faith in his salvation must fill our hearts and mouths, spilling out on each other every day. Without faith it is impossible to please God. *Faith IS the assurance of things hoped for the evidence of things not seen.*

I heard one brother speak of the "error of emphasis" and believe that this is partially the cause of the dilemma facing us today. Simply defined this is putting more emphasis on something that God is doing than he puts on it. We may not think this is serious but it is. *I refer to the type of "speaking the truth in love" permeating the Church today that causes people to look at themselves 99 percent of the time and at Jesus 1 percent of the time.* **God's emphasis is for us to look at Jesus 99 percent of the time and at ourselves 1% of the time!** If we do not, we gain a distorted view of God and misrepresent him. *The pain of division that racks the Body of Christ today is largely due to the amount of time we spend looking at ourselves instead of Jesus.*

Obviously we must confront sinfulness, but with the "good news". How many of us remember what the good news is? If we do then why do we change the rules for the believer? Ern Baxter said he was not ashamed of the Gospel (good news) for it was the power of God for salvation ... and if it is THE power then there is no *the'er* power, IT'S THE POWER! In our striving for excellence, we would do well to remember this. We do not have the ability to effect change in each other that is acceptable to God. It is his good news alone that can do this. At best, we may have the privilege of being His instrument.

Chapter 6

NOW THAT IS THE TRUTH! Remember, Jesus is the Gospel of God!

Proclaiming such a message seems utterly foolish to the natural mind. We must remember that it is the foolish things that God uses to confound the wise. While the scripture declares that we should all be fools for Christ it also says of the Romans, *"Although they claimed to be wise, they became fools and exchanged the glory of the immortal God for..."* You fill in the blanks. They traded God for images. Have we exchanged him for prestige or reputation? In our desire to be wise many have become "fools" and have actually done more damage than good.

We can become pharisaic proselytizers easier than we think and turn those seeking to enter the kingdom of God into twice the *"sons of hell"* we are. I believe the phrase; *"sons of hell"* could more accurately be defined as the "proponents of the law". A proponent is someone who supports and promotes something actively. This is not written to everyone who reads it. To those preachers of God's gracious good news I say, "Well done." Never stop proclaiming the finished work of Christ that those seeking to enter in may do so. To you who have fallen into Satan's age-old trap and have mistakenly perverted the good news, **BEWARE!**

If you have taken pleasure in what is seen rather than in what is in the heart, take heed, for you too will stand before the judgment seat of Christ that you may receive your due reward for what you have done while in the body. Will he merely wipe the tears from your eyes as you gaze at the ones who were brought into bondage by your message? Or will there be overwhelming joy filling your heart as you gaze at those who gained entrance to the everlasting kingdom through your proclamation of the Gospel? It is a feeling and privilege beyond compare to know that you have been a vessel used by the living God!

I urge you, as does Paul, *"So from now on we regard no one from a worldly point of view.... Therefore if anyone is in Christ HE IS a new creation; the old has gone, (no matter what it looks like) the new has come."* Stop trying to change people and proclaim God's change if you want to see true change! It was the love of Christ that compelled Paul to proclaim this good news without any distortion.

It is God-consciousness, not sin-consciousness that has the power to transform the unbeliever and the Christian alike. Looking at Jesus, not ourselves is the petition of scripture! What does the type of truth you speak cause people to do? Speaking His truth in love will cause us all to grow up into Him who is the head. From God's point of view, this will prepare the Bride for the wedding supper. It will clothe her in Christ's salvation and remove the stains of self-righteousness, pride and division that keep her from the banqueting table.

What Jesus builds from the inside out will stand in the Day of Judgment. What we build from the outside in will be utterly consumed in the fire. Our over-emphasis on "becoming" the perfect example of what New Testament Christianity should be, individually and corporately, has created a desire and obsession to put forth the veneer of a good reputation. However, God desires truth in the inward parts not truth that produces only external change. Christ made himself of no reputation!

In closing, it is my desire to speak the truth in love to those who have forgotten that our salvation is good news. I want to remind you that the kingdom of God is righteousness, peace and joy in the Holy Spirit. People who build from God's point of view quickly work themselves out of a job. There will always be a need for leaders to lead people to Jesus by proclaiming the truth of his Gospel, but not much need for constant oversight of the same people if they have been solidly espoused to the Lamb. If you can hear his voice you can follow him. People who build from a worldly point of view put themselves in a place of control and strive to become invaluable. Their followers become inordinately dependent on them instead of developing a healthy dependency on Jesus.

The King, not the kingdom, is our one vital need! True change brought about by the power of the Gospel not imposed structures, visions and causes must become our pursuit. If you would confront someone with what you call truth, make sure it is God's truth! Often we can become enslaved by "a" truth but we will always be set free by "the" truth! Jesus alone, is the way, the TRUTH, and the life! *"So from now on we regard no one from a worldly point of view."*

Satan's chief weapon is deception. His modus operandi was to imitate the old man. Speaking to these new children of God persistently in the first person, he eventually filled them with sufficient unbelief. They began to doubt themselves and God's salvation. Satan had found the landing strip he needed to launch his assault against the Bride of Christ. As God's children began to believe that Satan's thoughts and desires were their own a veil began to form once again in the temple. Much of our theology today only adds layers to this veil increasing its opacity. Much of what we call speaking the truth in love is anything but the truth.

I urge you to begin to agree with the words and work of God daily. If anyone were in Christ, he is a new creation. Whenever I meditate on God's salvation tears come to my eyes. The mouth of the Accuser of the Brethren is silenced and a voice within me begins to cry out, "I really do love God and want to serve Him."

The revelation that those vile lusts and evil desires might be coming from a source other than me releases the delivering hand of God in my life and sets me free from the power of the enemy. I want to declare to you that the new creation or child of God is just like Jesus. In addition, once we can silence the Accuser's voice we will actually begin to see ourselves as God sees us. Allow Jesus to wash your feet right now and ask Him to reveal more of His salvation to you.

CHAPTER SEVEN

The Commands of God

For God, who said, "Let light shine out of darkness," made his light shine in our hearts to give us the light of the knowledge of the glory of God in the face of Christ.

2 Cor. 4:6 (NIV)

It was early morning and I found myself rising from a late night. It was one of those times that just seemed to find me doing something out of some hidden program deep within. Like the navigational skill of the "homing pigeon", something I was totally unaware of was calling to me. Lately I had been wondering if I really loved God. I was sure I did not love anybody or anything else very much, especially myself. My heart had been feeling much like a big lump of clay or an old log, fallen long ago in some primeval forest, never to be seen by human eyes, as it returned to the soil of its birth.

Almost robotically, I found myself getting a cup of coffee and my old guitar. Finding my way in the darkness to the family room I took a sip from the mug and opened the guitar case. Even though the guitar had been sheltered by the case I could still feel the dust of disuse covering it. As I began to strum and tune I thought, how far away God seemed. I felt as though this would just be another exercise in futility. I began to play an old favorite called "Faithful One" but my voice was not awake yet so I went from singing to a whistle-hum to accomplish the vocal accompaniment. After a few choruses, a song I wrote not to long ago in a moment of inspiration came to mind. As I began to sing the words, something began to happen to me that was quite wonderful. (It should be noted that all the songs I write are for my personal times of worship and I have published none of them).

**Your Name is beautiful
Far above all names
and at the sound,
the Angels sing your Praise.**

**Your Name is Jesus
Far above all names
and at the sound,
the Heavens pour forth rain.**

**For in Your Name the blind can see
and in Your Name the prisoners are set free
In Your Name the lame can walk,
the deaf can hear, and the mute can talk.**

**Your name is Jesus
Yeshua too, Yesu or Hesus
they all speak of You
Your name is beautiful**

**Far above all names
and at the sound
the Angles sing Your praise!**

After the second time through the reality of what I was singing hit me and I began to sob. Sobbing was the *something wonderful* that happened. When I feel like an old lump of clay dryness is my closest friend. These tears were like rain from Heaven breaking a deadly drought I was hardly cognizant of. Until the tears came I had only wondered fleetingly why I felt so little love for anyone or anything, but now I was remembering whom the source of all love was. I was aware of the Angels in the room that had been doing exactly what I had just sung about and that the Savior to whom their praises were going was there! I do not remember what chain of thought led me into the revelation that Jesus shared with me that morning but, on that day I fell in love with **The Commandments** of God. Jesus was again showing me how important it is to stop trying to accomplish in my strength, what he had already accomplished through his marvelous life. This was to be another step into the *rest* of God.

In Psalm 119 David says he runs in the path of God's commands, because God has set his heart free. David also declared how he loved the law of the Lord, something I had to admit that I did not share with him. In fact, I had been grateful that Jesus had come because; I thought grace meant, He did it all so I would not have to do it at all. Then Jesus began to tell me that His name was more than just Jesus, or

Yeshua but He was also the Word of God, the Law of God, and the Commandment of God.

He said to me, "Cannot the God who commanded the light to shine out of the darkness also command a creative action into your heart. You have not been given the *will* in order to fulfill my commands in any strength of your own but my commands empower your will, which then becomes the force of your life. The will is the spiritual stomach that feasts on the Bread of Life. Though I have many names I am not divided, rather, I am One!"

The fulfilling of the commandments of God are not just things we do or don't do but they are a person we cling to with a tenacious loving embrace. Just as the resurrection is not just a day but the Son of God. In addition, revival is not just a time or season but the Holy Spirit, so the commands of God are not just things to do or not do; they are the empowering person of Christ living in our will, being who he is. Apart from Him, Jesus declared, we can do *no-thing*.

Just as God, had commanded the light to shine out of the darkness, and there was light. Jesus was telling me again, that all, not some of God's words are commands. A command, from the human point of view is something to be feared and obeyed, if we have enough intestinal fortitude. However, God's commands, from His perspective, are the way He creates. He is a creator and His commands are prophecy and fulfillment. The scripture is replete with instances of God and Jesus speaking and their commanding or creative words creating and bringing the proclamation to pass. Jesus told us that the words that He spoke were spirit and life.

I was beginning to see light at the end of the tunnel. No wonder David loved the law of God so much. God's ways were not hidden from him. I began to cry out repeatedly, "Father I receive your commands!" "Father I receive your commands!" I thought of the first command, especially in light of my recent doubts as to whether I truly loved God. *"You shall love the Lord your God with all your heart, and all your soul, and all your mind, and all your strength."* "Father I receive your commands!" "Father I receive your commands!" The tears began to flow again as the burden of failure was being washed away in the power of God's command.

Peter asked Jesus to command him to walk to Him on the water. Peter knew that if it were Jesus, His words would keep him afloat. As Peter stepped out of the boat, the Lord's words kept Peter afloat. It was not until Peter averted his gaze to the foaming sea that he began to sink. When Peter cried out for Jesus to save him the Lord did not rebuked him for not having enough faith to stay afloat, but for believing for one moment that Jesus wouldn't save him.

Can you see why it is so important that we keep our eyes fixed on Jesus? Can you see why the devil wants to avert our gaze? Nothing is more important than understanding our God's ways. He is a creator and he creates something from nothing with his words. Therefore it is critical that we believe and receive what he says is true in his Word about us, and not what the traditions of men proclaim as his truth. The difference is not hard to detect. Man's way is a constant struggle but Jesus' yoke is easy and his burden is light.

May God grant us the understanding of Peter, who knew that the ability to do what God asked of him, rested within those very words. Can you understand what Scripture means when it declares, "You have heard the Word but it has not profited you because it was not mixed with faith?"

Jesus answered, *"It is written: 'Man does not live on bread alone, but on every word that comes from the mouth of God.'"* (Mat 4:4)

Father, speak to me, I receive your commands! May the pages of your Bible shine with the new light of understanding granted only to God's children. It is my prayer that through meditation on God's Word, that the power of God's Word will more than fill your need.

CHAPTER EIGHT

Affliction—*Good or Bad?*

"Many are the afflictions of the righteous, but the Lord delivers them from them all."

Psalm 34:19 NKJV

Why we seem to suffer affliction is partly a mystery. Jesus rejoiced over God revealing certain mysteries to his disciples because they were "babes" and hiding them from the "wise". Many of the mysteries that enshroud God's plans and purposes for a generation await a simple childlike people to unlock them. It is the "babes" that Jesus gave power to, over the enemy. Like never before, we need power over the enemy. Jesus must have a Church that is truly fit for HIS use if he is to reach a lost and dying world, held captive by the deceptive power of Satan.

I want to take a moment at the outset of this writing to clarify one extremely important point and that would be the difference between affliction and sickness/disease. Today we see numbers of Christians suffering from cancer, diabetes and a host of other maladies. I do not believe in any way that God is glorified by our suffering these things. In fact, it is quite possible that the opposite is true. As one who has suffered from the effects of diabetes resulting in the amputation of four toes, a quintuplet heart bypass and surgery to remove my gall bladder, I know somewhat of which I speak. Lately, I have been going through a personal crisis of faith and loosing quite a bit of sleep over it, trying to reconcile the goodness of our God with the events of my life.

Just the other night as I sat waiting on the Lord, mainly because I could not sleep, certain Scriptures came to my mind. *The thief comes only to kill, steal and destroy, but I have come that you might have life and have it abundantly.* I said to the Lord, "This life that I am living is certainly not abundant." Then I recalled other Scriptures like John's inquiry in prison. *Are you the one we look for or is it another.* Jesus' reply was for John's disciples to go tell him how the blind received their sight, the deaf their hearing, the lame walked, the dead were raised and the Gospel was preached to the poor. One of the missions of Jesus was to redeem a misconception of his Father. To do this *he went about doing good and healing all that were oppressed of the devil, for God was with him!* He came to destroy the works of the devil.

As I continued in these thoughts, I went back to the words of Isaiah, how Jesus bore our *sickness and disease in his own body one the tree and by his stripes we were healed.* If he bore my sickness and disease in his own body how could I bearing my own sickness and disease in my body bring him glory? All one has to do is watch the movie The Passion by Mel Gibson to get a reminder of how brutal the beating was that Jesus took to secure our healing! I began to see how easily we can be duped by the deception of the devil into thinking that there is some value to our suffering sickness for his glory. I began to repent of a warped perception of our loving God and cry out for his forgiveness. As we will see, affliction is much different and should be distinguished from sickness and disease.

While the Word of God is perfect our interpretations often leave much to be desired. We may assume that most interpretation is on safe ground when it directs its reader to fix their gaze upon Jesus. The opposite is true when it causes us to turn our eyes from Jesus onto ourselves. That is not to say that we should never take a personal inventory, but morbid introspection does not benefit anyone.

One of the most subtle, and treacherous interpretations of God's Word suggests that we should develop "Godly" character. How can we develop what is already perfect. We simply need to become partakers of his character through the indwelling Holy Spirit. The former is not a new doctrine; in fact it predates Christianity, having its roots in Judaism. Mingled with the gospel of Jesus Christ it becomes an intoxicating, yet deadly potion, replacing God's righteousness with self-righteousness. It's greater danger lies in the distorted perspective of God it develops in its adherents. It portrays God as a stern and often unfeeling teacher. Never, through the words spoken, only through the subtle and haunting implications. He allows one trial after another to come upon us to somehow, through the affliction, make us better. Life seems to become one great exam that leads us "around the mountain" again and again, until we get it right. *We, not God, become the central theme of our existence.* Sometimes God redeems this understanding by allowing us to see what we are truly like. However, he does not need to test us for gaining knowledge about us. With the full knowledge of what we are and were, he gave his life for us.

Our heavenly Father does not keep records of our failures to hold us back. It is not our successful passing of one of his exams that moves us on to the next grade level. Jesus has already passed every exam that can be given. Jesus, not us, has already won the victory. Our task is to see through the trials that confront us into the riches of God's victory and provision.

In our desire to live lives that are problem free, many have assumed that a problem free life was a sign of God's blessing. I have come to believe that this is not true. Several years ago I heard a song that said, "... if I never had a problem I wouldn't know God could solve them..." If we did not have to face the problems that exist in a fallen world we would pat ourselves on the back and take all the credit for our "care-free" existence. We would never know God or He would be all too easily forgotten.

The trials we encounter in this life give God the opportunity to reveal himself. I believe faith is simply spiritual vision. Faith not only allows us to see God, for who he truly is, but enables us to enter immediately, the shelter of his presence. Why we try to treat faith as some spiritual commodity is beyond me.

We must remember that God is a Father. Unlike some earthly fathers, he desires to be in a personal relationship with his children. Faith is a doorway into our loving heavenly Father's presence, which nothing can shut. So often, we try to use the "key" of faith to unlock the ministry doors of deliverance, healing, and evangelism. However, this key only fits the door to our Father's heart.

Smith Wigglesworth, a famous man of God, put it this way. Once he was asked to pray for a very wealthy and influential woman who was near to death. As he entered her home, he felt the presence of Satan. When he went into the woman's room, he found her surrounded by her servants. As Smith knelt at the foot of her bed, the woman began to levitate above the bed. One of her servants asked Smith if he had the faith to deal with their master's (Satan) power. Smith's reply was humble and shocking. *"No,"* he said, *"but I have faith to get into my Master's presence and there He will give me, everything I need to deal with your master!"*

"That's just fine and dandy Jim," you say. "Then why have trials at all?" James said that faith without works is dead. God will not allow our faith to remain in the realm of intellectual knowledge only. ***"You believe in one God, you do well. The demons believe also and tremble!"*** Trials and afflictions are opportunities for God to prove his powerful love and salvation to everyone. The convenient part about all this is, with an antagonist like Satan, God will never run out of opportunities, if only we will see through the eye of faith and hope.

Chapter 8

When David was, a young Shepherd boy God allowed a lion and a bear to come into his life. I am sure these encounters were not sought after experiences among the shepherding community. Nevertheless, they confronted David just as the "lions" and "bears" of our modern day confront us. They may dress in the clothing of homelessness or job layoff or disguise themselves as a crippling injury or disease. However, they are not unlike the bear or lion of David's day. God is no less able or desirous of delivering us than he was David.

It was the lion and bear in David's life that prepared him for Goliath. Later when Saul pursued David, Ahimelech, the priest sought the Lord for him, gave him supplies and the sword of Goliath the Philistine. I believe when David looked at the sword he remembered the faithfulness of God and received the endurance he needed to hold out until God gave him the kingdom. God could have led David down a path with much less strife and tribulation, but God was preparing David to be King. To be an effective and benevolent King he had to know the power and love of God.

Ezekiel talks about a river coming out of the sanctuary and about wading in ankle deep then knee deep then up to the waist. As I thought of this I imagined how refreshing it is to wade in water. Then I envisioned myself going deeper and deeper into the water. Slowly I began to notice the power of the river. It was far stronger than I was. I soon realized I wanted to maintain control. Fear and apprehension began to set in, as I was just able to touch the bottom with my toes. The current was getting stronger and I knew I had come to a point of decision. Would I fight the river and try to make it back to the familiar territory of shallow water or go with its powerful flow?

Once I was swimming in the Rio Grande River along the border between Victoria, Texas and Mexico. I was overtaken by a similar experience and found myself trying to struggle to safety. I reached out, grabbed the overhanging roots of a tree, and experienced a temporary moment of relief. As the water cleared from my eyes I was looking into the face of a thirsty Tarantula, which was probably the largest in existence. Whether my arachnophobia had anything to do with my size estimation meant little to me at that point and the river quickly became preferable. I quickly devoted all my strength to helping the river carry me along its chosen course. Soon, to my delight, the river brought me to a shallow part and I walked out onto a beautiful sandy shore. Sometimes the greater test of faith can be surrendering yourself into the hands of the Lord rather than into the hands of the medical physician. Especially, when all your loved ones are telling you to make a wise choice and that wisdom would dictate that you should follow their advice. This is a very delicate subject so I would like to use another story to illustrate my point.

I will use the life of Smith Wigglesworth again. He had a very painful condition, which required him to take a medication of the day called salts. He was challenged to stop taking them and to trust the Lord. Finally, after believing he had received a word from God, he announced that he would stop taking them. He said that by tomorrow this time he would be suffering greatly from the lack of his medication, but he would rather die in faith than to live in fear. Well, the outcome was his deliverance and healing and an incredible miracle ministry that followed him everywhere with the proclamation of the Gospel. If you are facing a similar choice, you too, need a word from God to release faith in you. You too must come to the point that Smith did when you can say honestly, "I would rather die in faith than live in fear any longer."

Trust is what Lordship is all about—truly relinquishing control of your life. Allowing the river to take you where it wants can be a terrifying experience to those who do not know the love of their Heavenly Father. We want desperately to hold the mastery of our future under our own control. We just do not want to admit it. It isn't until a situation comes along that is beyond our control that the truth comes out. As we squirm and wriggle to free ourselves from the "hook" of dependency on God, our true spiritual state is revealed all too clearly.

"He always comes through," one person said, "I just wish he wouldn't wait so long." How many times I have thought I just can't continue to live like this. I am a nervous wreck. If that sounds like you then you, as I did, desperately need the message of God's hope written on your heart. Our children never worried about their provision, they knew that mommy and daddy would take care of everything.

Not long ago I felt the Lord say to me that the next thing he wanted to teach us about was hope. The word hope appears over sixty times in the New Testament. It can often be found in the company of faith and love. It is the Greek word *ELPIS* and means favorable and confident expectation—the happy anticipation of good.

It only makes sense that the devil would like to use the circumstances and situations of this life to steal hope. He comes to steal, kill and destroy. When we have no hope left, we have no reason to continue to live. Like no other time in history, the Church needs to nurse herself back to health on the hope of God. Then and only then can she proclaim his Gospel to the world!

I do not want to digress too much; however, I want to wed hope and faith, as the trials of life perfect them through a demonstration of God's love. The Word says that hope is the anchor of our soul. We have lived in the Chesapeake Bay area and have spent a lot of time on the water. One of the most important things on board a boat is the anchor. In cloudy weather, you cannot tell which way you are going. Without a compass, it is better to throw your anchor overboard and wait for a break in the weather. Through all the storms of life, when we seem lost and do not know what is going on, hope in God will always see us through. ***"Which hope we have as an anchor of the soul."***

In January of 1992, I was diagnosed with type 2 diabetes. I believed God said I would be healed. I based my hope on what I felt God was speaking to me during that period. The scripture says that Abraham, ***"who against hope believed in*** *hope, that he might become the father of many nations; according to that which was spoken."* The KEY was hope in what God had said. To date I have still not received the manifestation of God's word, but remembering who our God is sustains my hope.

Believe means to cling to. Both Abraham and I clung to hope. We clung to what God said even though we could not see it that we might both become what God said we would become. Abraham the father of many nations and me healed. Praise the Lord, who is the God of all hope.

We all hope for a better life, a raise, a better job, and a job period. We hope it does not rain on Saturday. We hope we will catch our quota during rockfish season. Alternatively, we hope that next year we will be able to take a family vacation. As Christians, hope takes on a completely new meaning. The scripture says that God calls things that are not as though they are. My children tried that from time to time and as parents, we called it lying. One major difference between my children and our God is, it is impossible for God to lie. God sees the end from the beginning. When he says something is going to happen you can *take that to the bank!*

Our challenge is to allow the hope that God *gives* us to become that needed anchor, when circumstance and situation would lie to us about the character of Christ. (*Now our Lord Jesus Christ himself, and God, even our Father, which hath loved us, and hath given [us] everlasting consolation and good hope through grace, Comfort your hearts, and establish you in every good word and work.* 2 Thes. 2: 16, 17) I believe God wants to change the way we view the daily circumstances and situations that confront us, radically.

Jesus wants us to begin to see every disaster as an opportunity for God's deliverance, and every handicap as an opportunity for God's healing. *"For this purpose the Son of God was manifested, that he might destroy the works of the devil."* Whenever we encounter the devil's "handiwork" hope declares, nay screams, LOOK, another chance for the Son of God to be manifested. Hope not only causes its owner to see life in a different way, but also unlocks the life of another kingdom. It brings the power of the age to come to bear against the devil's kingdom of deception and allows faith to open the doorway to victory. Victory is what our beautiful Savior sealed with his precious blood and his resurrection from the dead. Hope stares insurmountable odds in the face and laughs aloud. Hope looks at "Goliath" and only sees how small and helpless he is next to Jehovah!

"And every one that has this hope in them purifies themselves, even as he is pure." Once when we were going through a real financial crisis it became almost impossible to believe that God could, would or wanted to do anything about it. After some soul searching, we had a family discussion that revealed how much worry is the opposite of hope. By worrying, we were really saying we had no hope that God could change our situation.

By saying that, we were thinking things about our loving heavenly Father that were utterly unworthy of him. We knew that repentance was in order. As the Holy Spirit began to convict us and we sought forgiveness we noticed hope began to return. It was only a few days later that I began to work full time again. Hope in God has a guarding and purifying effect on the believer.

Whenever an overwhelming problem confronts us we should see it as one more chance for God to reveal his goodness. It is the goodness of God that leads to change. Education changes and shapes our minds. I know of no better definition of repentance. Hope in who our God is and how he feels about us will not disappoint us. God's love (which is a demonstration of his care for his children) has been and will be poured out on us.

Name the problem "bear" or "Lion" that confronts you right now and the love of God will find expression in the answer to that problem. If it is a crippling illness, His love will find expression in healing. If it is a lost job, his care will find expression in provision. If it is deep emotional pain because of abuse of any kind, his warmth and power will find an outlet as the One who restores your soul. If it is bondage to drugs, alcohol or pornography, his holiness will find expression as the One who sets the captives free.

I have talked about **faith** as being spiritual eyesight and the doorway into the presence of our loving Heavenly Father. I said that **hope** is the way we look at trials and tribulation, seeing them as opportunities for the Son of God to show his love. I said that **love** is a demonstration of God's nature in power to overcome and bring us through the trials and tribulations of our lives. Our Father delights in showing himself strong on our behalf. **These are the true keys to the Kingdom!** Just as these keys were a gift to Peter so they are our gift from God as well.

Many of us have allowed the events of life to speak evil of our loving heavenly Father. As a result, the Church is in crisis. Some of us have thought we could make ourselves better or more acceptable to God if we stoically endured and suffered patiently through these circumstances, all the while secretly believing God took some mysterious pleasure in it. However, no people have ever been able to rise above their conception of God. The most important thing about us is what comes to mind when we think about our God.

Our challenge is to remember that God is good and there is NO hurtful way in him. He is light and in him, there is NO darkness at all. Let us unclog the "conduit of our mind" with the truth of his Word, and allow the purity of his love and power to flow freely once again. Drink deeply of the sweetness of our God and use **the keys of the Kingdom** to unlock the gates to the age to come.

This is probably the greatest challenge facing the people of God — to reject the lies of the enemy and to take God at His word. And to dare to believe that He is truly as wonderful and merciful as His Word declares Him to be! *"Having done all to stand — STAND!"*

"Many are the afflictions of the righteous, but the Lord delivers them from them all."

Palm 34:19

CHAPTER NINE

FRIENDSHIP—*The Tie That Binds?*

"One will put a thousand to flight, two will put ten thousand to flight and a threefold cord is not easily broken."

(Ecclesiastics 4:12 KJV)

For such a long time I echoed th cry of David thinking, **"There is none that cares for my soul."** I assumed if I were part of a church that would be the job of the Pastor. I had even been a Pastor and tried to care for the souls of others knowing that if I would sow care I in turn should reap care. Over the years I have come to see things differently. I believe the Pastor is simply someone who leads us to the pasture; there he shows us where we can find grazing land. It is our role to eat.

Caring is not just an act of ministry, like correcting someone when they are doing something unscriptural or wrong. Caring is that intangible and mystical joining of one human soul to another in a way that fills you with desire and longing to meet all that persons needs that God will allow you to meet. It is difficult to define, in objective terms, something that goes beyond our ability to understand with our intellect, reaching down into the depths of our beings to bring wholeness. But, this is what friendship does.

A number of years ago, while spending time with the Lord, I thought of my first and best school friend, Tommy. We did everything together. It was quite a special time in my life. Many of us can think back to how special their first "real" friend was. Yet if your life is anything like mine the years has found that friendship betrayed or simply washed away. Time has found our hearts building up walls against similar experiences, and we have never found another friend like our first friend.

Suddenly something happened to me in that time of loneliness that was the beginning of one of the greatest changes of my Christian life. Jesus spoke to me and told me he was *"a friend that sticks closer than a brother."* In the atmosphere of all the memories of my first friendship, Jesus became my friend. He filled the need in me for the kind of friendship we all long for.

Then over the next few months, what usually happens with a word that brings me such excitement happened, it wore off. No matter how hard I sought to have the same experience again *it* was nowhere to be found. Little did I know that the word and experience was a seed that Jesus had planted deep in my heart? He needed to cover it up so that it could develop strong roots and grow into a tree of life within me.

Shortly after that we moved to Pasadena, where God renewed some old relationship. It was here among so many old, fond memories, that Jesus began to bring back the word he had planted two years before. I have often contended that the ministry of a prophet was the ministry of Jesus the Prophet through a man or woman to His people. The example follows for the Pastor and Evangelist, Apostle and Teacher and all the Gifts of the Spirit. A man I once knew said it best; "salvation is simply allowing Jesus to be Jesus in you." The question we should ask is not if the "five-fold" ministry is still the available today, but is Jesus still involved in the lives of his people.

I never had any problem grasping this concept as it related to ministry. Yet for some reason I never thought of friendship as a manifestation of the life of Jesus as well. I was beginning to realize how much Jesus longed to be a friend to me and through me when I realized it is the most important aspect in his relating to us. It is the foundation for the true release of these ministries.

When someone in the Church wants to get you to change or feels you may be moving in a wrong direction they usually quote a scripture to you like, *"faithful are the wounds of a friend,"* feeling this somehow qualifies them to speak into your life. A couple (couple "A") I know experienced just such an episode. They received a letter from another couple (couple "B") they had not seen in almost 12 years. The above verses, quoted in the letter, apparently made them (couple "B") feel they had the right and were qualified to address areas of perceived need in couple "A", setting them straight. I call this gross presumption at best. Unfortunately, the ones who really need "wounding" are usually the ones doing the wounding.

However, unlike "couple A's" "friends", our friend Jesus was wounded for our transgressions and bruised for our iniquities. The faithfulness of his wounds brings forgiveness and healing. They give him the right to speak into our lives and are the foundation of our relationship with him. How many of us can make that claim with those we desire to "set straight"? So many times we are simply responding to a personal offense, a bruised ego or worse, seeking to protect some personal domain, vision or kingdom that we did not bleed or die for. Too many times our motives are our motives and not the motives of Jesus – the friend!

I remember a prophecy someone once gave me that said because of my "prophetic" calling God would often allow me to see the weaknesses of my fellow Christians. However, I would hardly ever be called to do anything more about it than pray for them. There is a lot of wisdom in those words. We would all do well to heed them.

In our society we have watered down the word friendship. My children used to come home from Sunday school every week telling me of another friend that they have made. Yet scripture declares that friends are few. Friendship is a gift from God, and a supernatural experience, initiated by God. God is love and as we partake of his divine nature, his presence allows us to become friends. Jesus is "THE FRIEND" and the source of all true friendship. We cannot be a friend until we become one with the friend! We must learn to allow Jesus to be Jesus in us.

Jesus wants to manifest himself as "the friend" to those he will use to spearhead this next move of his Spirit and he will not settle for anything less, because we reproduce what we are and relationships of love, fervent love are what matters to him. All the signs, wonders and miracles are nothing for him to do, but to so fashion the heart of man or woman into a vessel that truly reflects the substance and passion of his love and being is a true and extraordinary work of the Spirit.

I must confess that in most of my relationship there comes a point when I put up my walls to protect myself against the pain of what I believe will inevitable—abandonment. I need to learn how not to fear Christ's love in me, because he is willing to suffer denial, betrayal and even death for those who even hate and despitefully use him. I want desperately to have the kind of friendship that can only come from the manifestation in our lives of Jesus the friend.

I believe that the longing in our hearts for friendship is really God's longing. He formed us out of the dust of the earth and breathed his Spirit into us. Then because of his great longing, he made himself a body that he might live with us, walk with us, hold us and be our friend.

Yet, his plan did not stop there. His capacity to love and care for us is beyond measure. His friendship was so great he demonstrated his own words, ***"no greater love has any man*** *than he lay down his life for his friends."* After his resurrection, he could live in the hearts of countless millions over a hundred generations expressing his loving friendship. He calls us no longer servants but friends because he has shown us what he is doing. Friendship is as supernatural and miraculous as deliverance, and divine healing. Friendship is as much a manifestation of Jesus' ministry as that of the apostle, pastor or prophet.

I believe Jesus spends most of our Christian lives healing, restoring and purifying our souls so that he can pour himself through us as "the friend" that loves at all times. This is what scripture calls the end of our instruction. This is the sign of a mature faith. Once these friendships are formed he can then begin to release the "ministry of example" to a starving world that will declare, "See how they love one another." *"By this shall all men know that you are my disciples that you have love for one another."* In case we have forgotten God's definition of love we might want to take a moment to read it again.

Here is a scriptural definition of love from 1 Corinthians 13:4-8 *"Love is patient, love is kind. It does not envy, it does not boast, it is not proud. It is not rude, it is not self-seeking, it is not easily angered, it keeps no record of wrongs. Love does not delight in evil but rejoices with the truth. It always protects, always trusts, always hopes, and always perseveres. Love never fails..."*

We usually think of hate in only its vile or heinous terms when scripturally it is simply the opposite of LOVE. It is this misconception concerning what hate is that allows it to spread its venomous malignancy throughout the Body of Christ. If we viewed being unkind or not believing the best as hate we all might be a little more "friendly". Most of us through acts of omission or commission release this definition of hatred toward someone each day.

I feel we have stopped short of God's longing for our lives by putting anything above this kind of friendship. We are totally inadequate to make this happen. We need to cry out for God's mercy and goodness to do this in all our lives. We need to ask Jesus to purify our souls for the sincere affection of the brethren. The way Peter put it was, to give us a love for each other that was fervent (or heated white hot). We will be unable to experience this type of friendship until we see Jesus as our friend and source, until his priorities become our priorities. We must trade in our ambitions for greatness for his definition for greatness. His ambition for our lives is to make us friends.

My friend Tommy and I were almost inseparable. We met in a hallway in seventh grade, rolling on the floor as we traded blows. No one can remember what started the fight. From that point on there was no need to prove anything to each other. We simply loved and accepted one another. If one of us had money the other had money. We did not try to make each other feel poor or underprivileged. We shared everything from cars to heartaches. No matter what happened we were there for the other.

How special that first friendship is. It is a shame that everyone's first friend isn't Jesus. He is the only one who will never betray us or let us down. How hard it is to give the same depth of trust we so freely gave that first time, again. We must try not to fear friendship, and entrust our souls to Jesus. Tommy is gone. The outcome of his life is unknown by me. But Jesus, "...is the friend that sticks closer than a brother!" This is how he desires to express his life in us. The question before us, as we read this is, "are we willing to open up old wounds or receive new ones that the walls of self-preservation may be torn down within us? Are we willing to share in the fellowship of Christ's suffering that we may see the power of his resurrection? Will we allow Jesus to be Jesus in us?"

CHAPTER TEN

Acceptance—Selective or Unconditional?

Accept one another, then, just as Christ accepted you, in order to bring praise to God.

(Romans 5:17 NIV)

In 1987, two years after my mother's death, Terry and I moved the whole family to California. We were living in the high desert town of Lake Los Angeles, a suburb of Palmdale. Lake LA, as the residents like to call it, was in the middle of a construction boom that was soon to pop. At her peak, she could boast about 13,000 folks, a great many were employed in the aircraft industry. It was during this time we received a cassette tape in the mail. It was a radio broadcast by a Pastor from the area we had just moved from. His guests on the show were Charles and Dotty, some old friends of ours.

As I listened, something Dotty said struck a chord deep within my heart. **"We must create an environment where failure isn't fatal."** This would be an environment of unconditional acceptance. So often, the acceptable standard for behavior set by the Church does not allow for any shortcoming or failure. Or those who do fail become fatalities. When I speak of unconditional acceptance, I am speaking of the quality of acceptance Jesus showed us as unbelieving sinners. People who were his enemies and scoffed at him were the ones he died for. *In the full knowledge of all our sin and sinfulness, he shed his blood.*

How many of us have struggled with recurring sin at one time or another? Or secretly held resentment towards someone? How many times have we covered up a wound received at the hands of a brother or sister? We confess our dilemma to the Lord, but because of fear of what others might think we seldom confide in anyone or try to right a wrong. To our surprise it keeps coming back to haunt us like a specter in the night. Eventually there is a parting of the ways because there is not the freedom to talk things through. Finally, our heart becomes hard and we move into the "backslider" stage. Or guilt, self-condemnation and bitterness, inducts us into the ranks of the "spiritually handicapped".

Conditional acceptance is any level of acceptance we show toward each other that is less than the level of acceptance that Jesus has for us. Conditional acceptance produces fear of rejection. Fear of being rejected causes many to cover up their recurring sin. You notice I placed everything mentioned above, in the category of recurring sin. Failure to try and resolve any of the above situations is a failure to walk in love. Walking in love is God's number one command!

I am not suggesting an environment of unconditional acceptance of sin, but of the sinner. I am not speaking of the one who **refuses to admit their sin and forsake it.** I am **speaking of the** weak saint that has yet to understand, the victory of Calvary and the power of the blood of Jesus.

We must remember that Jesus has dealt with the problem of sin forever through the shedding of his blood. When it was accepted on Heaven's Altar for the remission of mankind's sin it became eternal in its efficacy. The problem before mankind today is not a sin problem but a sinner problem. How to transform the sinner into the image of God is the dilemma facing us today. Focusing on our sinfulness has absolutely no transforming value. Focusing on the finished work and person of Christ, and clothing each other in the robes of his righteousness, and unconditional acceptance however, has great transforming virtue.

We must stop trying to manipulate the transforming work of God in each other's lives through our "new laws". Conditional acceptance is designed to make others conform or perform according to our expectations, definitions or timetables. Instead, we need to, through the power of God's loving acceptance, create an atmosphere where Jesus can transform us into his image. We are now his, to do with as he pleases, not each other's.

At no stage in our Christian life does "good moral character" become an acceptable trade for "Godly Character". Many religions exhibit good moral character. At no point can we define spiritual maturity as the fruit of our endeavor, rather than the Fruit of the Spirit. The terrible force of rejection's destructive activity in our lives, no matter what the source, can only be healed by the endless, unconditional acceptance of God's love.   Actually, the only condition to *receive* this unconditional acceptance is faith in Jesus Christ.

Jesus is the same yesterday, today and forever. What he did for us when we first came to him, he does for us every minute of every day, throughout eternity! That is not "greasy grace," that is the Gospel. In my experience, it is the goodness of the Lord that produces true change in his children.   An environment where acceptance is selective breeds fear and only delays deliverance.

Paul was a man who knew the unconditional acceptance of God. The power of God's acceptance has shaped and molded every great man and woman of God in history. Paul never forgot his persecution of the Church. Peter never forgot his denial of Christ on the eve of his crucifixion. It was the memory of their wretched state in comparison with God's beauty and holiness that allowed His Spirit to make them great. Their condition apart from the work of Christ was settled forever in their minds. They had ceased striving to be better or to make anyone else better. They reveled in the finished work of Calvary and taught others to do likewise.

This final acceptance of our condition apart from God's covering and intervention eliminates "double-mindedness" and allows us to finally take our eyes off each other and ourselves and fix them on the only one who can change us, Jesus. We no longer know one another or ourselves after the flesh. We begin to see the finished work of Christ and it changes each of us.

Jesus said he would build his church and the gates of hell would not prevail against her. Our responsibility is to walk in the unconditional acceptance, love of Jesus Christ, and leave the assembly work to him. Many of us have been running with a vision we feel God has given us. In our excitement, we have forgotten who our God is. We have forgotten the one who came to serve and give His life as a ransom for others. We have forgotten the One who made himself of little reputation. We have forgotten the friend of sinners and harlots. We have forgotten that HE IS LOVE and has clothed us in a righteousness that needs no more perfecting. Once again we have averted our gaze from the only one worth looking at.

A friend of mine has a sign in his office that says, "The main thing is to keep the main *THING THE MAIN THING*." Who Jesus is and what he does is the "main thing"! Help create an environment where failure is not fatal and honesty, openness and acceptance can thrive. I guarantee we will all be the better for it. Remember Jesus accepts us accept one another also.

There are sins of commission and omission. Both defile and divide the Body of Christ. If we know that forgiveness is not an option and that we all miss the mark daily, we might all embrace a more gentle and restorative spirit.

Let us create an environment where failure is not fatal and love and acceptance permits the salvation of God to flow freely in our lives. An old axiom says, "together we stand, divided we fall." It must become more than a trite cliché, if we want to see the blessing God.

In every city in America there are war stories told of who is right and who is wrong in the divisions that have fraught the Church. I think it's time we all grew up and left the judgment to Him who judges righteously. It's time we dare to believe that He will perfect that which concerns every one of his children. The wheat and tares will be separated at the Harvest.

The rifts that exist between individuals and churches can be healed and overcome through our unconditional acceptance and love for each other. True acceptance recognizes our deep need for one another. In the war against Darkness, for the souls of men, we need all the love available. A basic military strategy is to divide and conquer. Let us create an environment where failure is not fatal and let us begin in our personal lives. You learning to accept you is the key to accepting others.

CHAPTER ELEVEN

The Blood Covenant of Christ

One morning I awoke with the Lord tying some thoughts together in my mind. I had just finished reading a book that had inspired me greatly. It was about the blood covenant of Jesus Christ. It spoke about the exchanges that take place in a blood covenant and how this particular covenant is an *unequal* covenant. It is called an unequal covenant because the responsibility for both parties fulfilling the terms of the covenant rests solely upon Jesus. As well, it was called an unequal covenant because blessing was given to us in the place of deserved cursing. Instead of deserved judgment, condemnation and eternal separation from God we receive mercy, reconciliation and the same quality of fellowship with God that Jesus experiences with his Heavenly Father. This is referred to as the exchange of life. God was speaking to me about this exchange of life in my state somewhere between dreaming and reality.

I was picturing the whip of the centurion lashing out at the back of Jesus. Every fiber of the whip was saturated with the sin and resulting sickness of body, soul and spirit of fallen humankind. Then certain scriptures would race through my mind at lightening speed as different pictures came. The words of the prophet

Isaiah flooded my thoughts:

> *His visage (or appearance) was marred more than all the sons of men so great was his disfigurement. ... He was wounded for our transgressions, bruised for our iniquities, the chastisement for our peace was upon him and by his stripes we were healed.*

Isa. 52:14; 53:5 (NIV Version)

For the first time I really began to understand what it meant that *by his stripes* I was healed. The centurions whip was taking the culminated sins of all humankind throughout all the ages and literally burning them into the flesh of Jesus. Just as a Jew would lay his hands on a sheep before he slit its throat, confessing his sinful life into it, so the cat of nine tails was confessing the sinful life, sickness and pain of all humankind into God's sacrificial lamb. With every stroke of the whip, we were becoming one with the Son of man, and he, one with us. All of humankind, the race of Adam, was coming to an end of life through Christ's death on the cross. Scripture calls Jesus the Last Adam. Somehow, Jesus was able to transcend the limitations of time, as we understand it, and bring all of Adam's, unborn race into himself on the cross. Jesus really is the first and the last.

Just as God once had put an end to life on planet earth with a great flood, now he was putting an end, finally, to Adam's race through his Son's death on the cross. When he rose up from the dead a brand new race of men and women that had never before existed rose up in him. They were those who had **put their hope in Israel's Messiah, and all those who would ever** believe in him, still unborn. We are the "born-from-above" ones. We are those born out of heaven by the Holy Spirit and the will of God, through the blood of Jesus. All of humankind with its sin, past present and future, was in Christ on the cross, and died when he did. Some have and will rise to newness of life here and now, and some will not. We who acknowledge this covenant will one day receive a glorified body, while those that do not will rise to stand in the judgment and receive eternal separation from God for their rejection of his covenant and his ways.

After Jesus rose from the dead, Mary did not recognize him until he called her name. Then he quickly told her not to touch him, because he had not yet ascended to his God and her God to his Father and her Father. This victorious Son of man was declaring to Mary her complete and new identity found in him. The Psalmist tells us that Angelic protectors shouting out the question challenged his resurrection procession into the Holiest Place in Heaven, *"Who is this King of Glory."* Neither Mary nor the Protectors of the Ancient Gates recognized the blood stained mutilated body that was getting ready to stand before Jehovah as the High Priest of a new race of beings. But as he stood before his Father to present himself as the atoning sacrifice his Father saw the suffering of his servant's soul and was satisfied. He stretched out his hand and ratified the new and everlasting blood covenant by transforming Jesus and the throng of the faithful that were with him into their glorious heavenly bodies. As they began his coronation to the highest seat of authority in the universe, joy began to sweep through heaven's host. They began to see the glorious Son of God revealed in the victorious Son of Man. It's no wonder Jesus came back to earth for forty days to explain what had and was going to happen as a result of his ultimate victory on the battlefield of Golgotha.

When Jesus healed the crippled man he said, *"Which is easier to say, 'Your sins are forgiven,' or to say, 'Get up and walk'? But so that you may know that the Son of Man has authority on earth to forgive sins...."* Then he said to the paralytic, *"Get up, take your mat and go home."* As I thought about what my answer would have been if Jesus had asked me that question, I felt the Spirit say to me, "Of course it is easier to *say* your sins are forgiven because it demands no demonstration or proof of forgiveness. Or does forgiveness of sin from my perspective of salvation require a demonstration of forgiveness?" As I thought about this incredible statement, it was as if the Holy Spirit were asking and answering the questions in my mind. "The salvation Jesus gives demands proof of forgiveness." The Spirit was drawing a correlation in my mind between all the healings and miraculous signs performed by Jesus, and the forgiveness of sin revealed in His gospel of salvation. When Jesus, who came to put sin away, said, *"But so that you may know that the Son of Man has authority on earth to forgive sins"* it became very clear that he was speaking as the one who would take this man's sin on himself and that was the basis of his authority.

Then I began to think about the time he was telling his disciples whoever sins they forgave would be forgiven and whose sins they retained would be retained. The reason Jesus could forgive sin was because it, along with all its devastating effects would be placed in him and die in him on the tree. "Just a minute Jim," you say, "Jesus was God, couldn't he do anything he wanted to do?" No, he could not. The Scripture says that without the shedding of blood there is no remission of sin. As the Judge of the whole earth, he had to condemn humankind justly to death because of their sinfulness. However, as the sin-bearer he could grant them forgiveness of sin and raise them up from the dead in him.

The reason his disciples were to share in his power to forgive sin and the subsequent healings, and miracles was that they were to be the tellers of the good news. Whoever responded to the blood covenant of Christ through their words would receive the obvious manifestations of God's forgiveness. When Peter saw that, the crippled man had faith he proclaimed Christ's forgiveness by telling him to RISE UP AND WALK! Peter understood, as did most of his contemporaries, the basic principles of a blood covenant and the exchanges that take place in the cutting of such a holy covenant.

The result of faith in the blood covenant of Jesus Christ is an absolute exchange of lives. Satan has deceived us into believing that sin is an act more than a state of being separated from God. I believe it is more a state of alienation from God which results in certain recurring "sinful" actions. However, to the one who understand God's ways the only logical outcome of God's salvation is the perfect restoration of the spirit, soul and body. When Jesus walked on the earth, he looked into the eyes of many who put their faith in him, and healed everyone who came to him. Christ's blood atonement is the basis for his forgiveness, and the manifestation of his forgiveness is healing and wholeness. Jesus desires to elevate those who put their trust in him to a new level of existence. Scripture declares that we were dead in our sins ... but now God has made us alive. It goes on to declare that God has translated us from the kingdom of darkness into the kingdom of his dear Son.

The Bible is not a book of dispensations; it is a book of Covenants. God's sovereignty does not make him whimsical and unpredictable. God has ways, they may not be like our ways but he desires to reveal them to us. He is steadfast, dependable, faithful and immutable. If we will give him the time to reveal himself to us we will find our God to be the only sure foundation this life has to offer. If we are to be apart of his covenant we must ask him to destroy any preconceived religious notions and doctrines that would rob it of its power and cry out for the Spirit of Truth to lead us and guide is into that for which God has apprehended us. Then let us serve up His Good News in a demonstration of the Spirit's power and not with mere words of men's wisdom.

Then he opened their minds so they could understand the Scriptures. He told them, *"This is what is written: The Christ will suffer and rise from the dead on the third day, and repentance and forgiveness of sins will be preached in his name to all nations, beginning at Jerusalem. You are witnesses of these things. I am going to send you what my Father has promised; but stay in the city until you have been clothed with power from on high."* (Luke 24:45-49 NIV)

CHAPTER TWELEVE

Supernatural, Natural or Spiritual, What Are We?

I had just been talking with my wife about our favorite subject, finances, when my youngest daughter, Katie interrupted. "Daddy could you pray for my ankle I think I sprained it?" A couple of years ago I would have offered *token* prayers or tried to get quickly into a *spiritual* frame of mind. I would have quoted a number of scriptures in order to try and work up enough *faith* to get enough *feeling* to believe God would listen and heal my little girl. However, today was different. I looked at Katie and said, "Come here, let's pray." As soon as I touched her ankle she declared, "Daddy I can feel the Holy Spirit touching me!" Immediately the pain left her ankle and she began to walk on it again. It was still a little stiff from the swelling but for the next few days, she would rejoice over her healing whenever she saw me.

What was the difference? What had changed? Certainly, God had not changed, His Word says, *"I the Lord do not change."* (Mal. 3:6 NIV) Certainly His Word did not change it is established forever. The only equation in my life's formula that had changed was ME! It was my transformed perspective of God, His Word and His intention for creation that allowed this new result to take place in my life. I am no different than any of God's children. He did not suddenly give me some special anointing for healing in the middle of a financial discussion. Or recently call me into some type of miracle ministry. I have struggled with all the same ailments and common everyday afflictions that plague humankind.

Then one day as I was reading a book the author made an interesting statement that provoked me to ponder something I had never really considered. He wrote, "The word *super-natural* does not appear in the Bible." I thought that can't be true, so I went to my trusty computer Bible and told it to search the entire Bible for the word *super-natural*. Its response confirmed my brother's statement, "There are no occurrences of the word *super-natural* in this translation. Do not get me wrong I am glad that such a word exists. Yet I think our God goes way beyond simply being elevated up the "natural scale" until he reaches the rank of super. God is a Spirit and the Father and Creator of all other spiritual beings. Yet God as a Spirit stands alone and is altogether unique. He is the only uncreated being in the entire Universe. So we can accurately say that there is no one, or nothing else like our God. He is absolutely different from anything else in all of creation.

For a moment, let us imagine that we have a time machine and we are going to go back into time. As we arrive in the most ancient of days we open the door to our time machine. Air rushes into our lungs that have never before been breathed by any other human being. As we look around, we see a beautiful primeval forest surrounding the most exquisite garden you can imagine. Through this garden flows a river that does not know the meaning of the word pollution. Crouching on its beckoning shoreline is the most resplendent being eyes will ever look upon. As we draw closer, we are overwhelmed with a sense of well-being. The love we discover coming from Him is expressed in the tender and caring manner with witch he is shaping and molding something. With soil from the banks of the river and water, he has fashioned and formed a figure that resembles him in basic shape and form. Then suddenly, when it appears that he kneels closer to admire his handiwork, the very air around becomes charged with some strange and unknown energy. For a moment, there is absolute silence, almost a feeling of reverence. It's as though an unseen host is anxiously waiting for what is going to take place next. As this resplendent being's face touches the face of his sculpture, he appears to be giving it mouth-to-mouth resuscitation.

We look around to make sure that nothing has escaped our gaze when unexpected movement catches our eye. This awesome creature of light is dancing on the shores of the great Euphrates River. Then, to our surprise, we see the sculpted form filled with life and mimicking the dancing of his new found Creator. The atmosphere has turned form still reverence into jubilant celebration, as Father and son gaze into each other's eyes.

Of course, most this is speculation but I can still see it in my mind. This resplendent spiritual form in our time travels is of course, God. The form fashioned and molded by him from the soil and water of the riverbank was Adam. However, it was the natural elements combined with the Spirit from our marvelous God that made possible the animated being known as *man*. The lifeless elements of the natural world married to the Spirit of God brought forth an offspring. The two became one flesh in Adam.

The Scripture speaks of a man and a woman becoming one flesh. Only recently did I realize that this was much more than just the consecration of the wedding bed. As I listened to a speaker talk about this as being God's prophetic blessing on the marriage bed, expressed in the fruit of the womb, my mind became ecstatic as I considered the other implications. My son, David, was not fully like his mother or me but in him my bride and I had become one.

Paul declares, ***"For this reason a man will leave his father and mother and be united to his wife, and the two will become one flesh. This is a profound mystery-but I am talking about Christ and the church."*** (Eph 5:31-32.) Our heavenly husband has chosen to wash His fallen earthly bride in his own blood. The consecration of their wedding vows produced a species of being that has not walked on the face of the earth since that day, in our imagined time travels, in the Garden of Eden. The one major, and significant difference between the fruit of that first union and the fruit of this new union is, we can never again be separated from the love of God that is in Christ Jesus our Lord. **Hallelujah!**

What does all this mean to us living in a practical everyday world? It means that the same relationship that was available to the first Adam is now available to us. If you are not a Christian put your trust in Jesus and the doors will open wide. Adam was fashioned by God to have his conscious awareness through God's Spirit in him. Everything that would enter Adam's through his five senses would be filtered through God's Spirit within him. God would **teach all of Adam's knowledge to him** personally. God would joyously supply every single need that would come into his life. In addition, through God meeting each need, Adam would get to know his Father a little better. Adam would see this glorious new world through its Creator's eyes. All of his natural needs would be known and met by spiritual forces. To Adam the spiritual world was as much apart of him as the natural. One was his mother the other was his Father. This child brought great pleasure to his parents. They were in total harmony in this innocent wonder.

I fear that the word *super-natural*, as much an integral part of our vocabulary as it is, has somehow erected a wall between our Heavenly Father and us. While he is Omnipotent and we are limited, he never meant for us to be impotent. My children do not have all of my characteristics but they have some of them, as they do their mother's. As *born again* children of God we can never posses all of our Uncreated, Omnipotent Father's power or characteristics, but we should have some. We, like Adam must learn who we are. Until we are as at home in the spiritual world as we are in the natural world, we have missed out on all that Jesus suffered and died to restore. It's time we were more than *"ma ma's" (natural) boys or girls* and allowed God to turn us into children of our Father (spiritual) who is in Heaven.

CHAPTER THIRTEEN

Freedom!

"Now the Lord is the Spirit, and where the Spirit of the Lord is there is freedom."

(2 Cor. 3:17 NIV)

"Villains who twirl their mustaches are easy to spot but those who clothe themselves in good deeds are well camouflaged." My mind began to wander as I listened to Captain Picard. He had just communicated a greater truth to his security officer, Mr. Warf, than he realized. Warf was a proud and duty bound Klingon who lived for honor and glory. As the plot of this episode unfolded Warf was getting caught up in the investigation of those involved in an alleged conspiracy against the United Federation of Planets. Reading between the lines of this plot one could see the author's desire was to expose the freedom or bondage that can be brought on a society through the ideals they embrace. As our plot develops, we find Simon Tarsus, the medical assistant, being persecuted and prosecuted for treason because of his contact with a confessed spy. The recently uncovered truth of his Romulan (enemies of the Federation) grandfather only fueled the fire his assailants sought to feed. At first glance, everything being done seemed like the right thing to do. However, like so many well-intentioned endeavors, this one was quickly turning into a witch-hunt.

When a confrontation arose between Captain Picard, the defender of the rights of man, and Lieutenant Warf, the advocate of the truth, things got a little tense. Warf's greatest redeeming factor is his willingness to confess his error when convincingly confronted. It is every Christian's privilege to preserve and proclaim the faith our Savior gave his life for. Yet, I fear in doing so many have turned this blessed privilege into a witch-hunt, leaving many poor saints burning at the stake. Church history is one endless road of persecution. Yet the uninformed reader may be surprised to know that there has been more persecution of the church, by the church than by the "heathen".

The reason we can find so many different Christian churches is the direct result of the persecution of the faithful by the faithful. Our price for freedom is vigilance. We must be ever vigilant and faithful to expose those who pervert the gospel and freedom the shed blood of Jesus Christ purchased for us. Unfortunately, as history has shown, the ones being persecuted were usually the true guardians of the gospel! A student of Church history could easily become distraught by the atrocities wrought for the *sake of righteousness* in the *name* of Jesus Christ.

Those who draw their security from constantly speaking of our Christian responsibilities to God and one another should be the subject of everyone's scrutiny. They often do so in order to see their vision of the Kingdom become a reality. Usually they know little of the freedom Christ's salvation brings. Many others call us to performance because they have not yet dealt with the scars and pain that motivate them at the core level of their beings. For us who have been saved by God's merciful grace through faith in his holy Son's sacrifice responsibility is better defined as *respondibility*. All we need to do to have God consider us as responsible children are to respond to His voice when He speaks.

The words that come from our heavenly father's mouth are certain to accomplish what they proclaim. Whether they are past tense, as promise in Scripture, or present tense, as a word impressed upon our hearts by his Spirit, they are alive. Time doesn't make God's word ineffectual-they are living and active. Jesus said that the words that he spoke were spirit and life. They were much more than simply the hollow sounds of air passing across the vocal chord of a fallen species.

His love for us compelled him to give himself over to the power of death, but it was not simply symbolic of his love. His death secured him the right to change those who came to him. Jesus isn't satisfied to die for us and leave us like we are. He transforms all those who put their trust in him by becoming one with them. He alone can do this and he does it in his own time and in his own way.

After his resurrection and ascension, he began to do just that by pouring out his Spirit on betrayers and cowards. Those who, just weeks before, had denied him now loudly proclaimed his name publicly. *"And we who with unveiled faces all reflect the Lord's glory, are being transformed into his likeness with ever-increasing glory, which comes from the Lord, who is the Spirit."* Whose glory are you reflecting? The greatest way to preserve the faith is to become just like its author. However, the ability does not lie within the realm of human effort. Christ is the only one with the ability to bring about this mysterious transformation. Mystery is a word used quite often in the Bible. God does not feel the necessity to apologize for his mysteries; neither does he feel the need to explain them. He simply asks us to believe that they are; and accept them in faith.

What savior, or hero for that matter, would give his life for the fair maiden (or in our case the not-so-fair maiden) just so the villain could seduce her after his demise? Jesus might have appeared to have been defeated at Calvary, but in reality he was the supreme victor. He never intended for anyone else to care for his redeemed. Jesus does not need anyone else to teach us his ways, nor can anyone else cherish his bride in the intimate fashion that he can. Our intense desire is to see children of God become what they claim to be, led of the Spirit. If it is the result of well-intentioned human concern, or ecclesiastical intimidation it is worthless. I do not believe that Scripture's entreaty for us to look on the needs of others was a license from God to begin changing each other. Rather, God's desire is for us to simply provide for each other's material and emotional needs.

Freedom!

No one can cure the naturally diseased state of the human heart but Jesus. Heart transplants don't have a 100% success rate in the natural, yet Jesus can give us a brand new heart, successfully, every time. When we learn to walk the path of faith in the faithfulness of God, we will walk on the pathway of freedom and power. Paul told us to follow him as he followed Christ. This kind of leadership is the only kind of leadership recognized in heaven. The small and insignificant titles men bestow upon themselves to satisfy their insecurities mean nothing to heaven. But, those who lead us by their example of intimacy with Jesus bring great joy to the heart of God.

"Now the Lord is the Spirit, and where the Spirit of the Lord is, there is freedom."

CHAPTER FOURTEEN

Kidnapped!

*For those God foreknew he also predestined to be conformed
to the likeness of his Son, that he might be the firstborn
among many brothers.*

(Rom. 8:29)

Many years ago I was attending a Christian festival called
"JESUS-78". As I listened to speaker after speaker, over a 3
day period, a deep concern was birthed in my heart. Turning
to a dear friend of mine I said, "This event is called *JESUS-78*
but no one is talking about Jesus." His reply came almost
rehearsed and too quickly, "Yes Jim, but if Jesus were here he
wouldn't be talking about himself." I thought to myself, "Yes,
but if Jesus were here in the flesh, he would be demonstrating
a quality of life so rich in love and power he wouldn't need to
speak about himself, everyone else would!" Since that time, I
have seen a *tsunami* of practical teaching overwhelm the Body
of Christ. The eventual outcome of causing anyone to be
preoccupied with anything but Jesus is a sterile form of
godliness. We slowly wean them from the pure milk of God's
life, and stick the lifeless pacifier of "religion" in their mouth.

Chapter 14

Through our deep and personal relationship with Jesus, each individual believer is taught and empowered by his Holy Spirit, to deny ungodliness and worldly lust. It is through that deep and intimate association alone that we can live a sober, righteous and godly life that is *acceptable* to God in this present world. I use the word acceptable because Paul, before his conversion, lived a *sober, righteous and godly life.* Yet, he persecuted the Church, imprisoned Christians, and consented to the stoning death Stephen and of many others.

Much of what is going on in Christianity today is not much more than a pacifier. This is written out of a deep Godly jealousy for the preeminence of Jesus and the salvation his blood and suffering purchased us.

When I first came to Jesus as a repentant sinner it was because I had already tried everything the world had to offer. I was still empty and dead inside. Money, drugs, sex, power, violence, yes, and even *Harley-Davidson* motorcycles could not fit into the empty space in my heart. God created the needs within humankind to be nourished by one thing only, **JESUS CHRIST!** Out of this relationship we would be able to give instead of take. The manifested life of God would fill one side of our new heart and steadily pump out his life from the other side of this new heart. This is what the natural and spiritual organ was designed to do. What a glorious and great salvation. If we actually possessed and imparted this kind of salvation, our children could not be fooled by the imitations the devil is constantly offering them.

Kidnapped!

The old saying that *variety is the spice of life* is at best only a half truth. The Devil dwells in the realm of half-truths and deception, offering humankind everything but the bread from heaven. His *"truths"* teach us to be users and abusers of humankind. We must heal all Satan oppresses if we are truly people who have Christ living in us.

When some "enter" the Kingdom of God, they feel great initial satisfaction. It's as if they have feasted for the first time. Then slowly over the months and years, the enemy enacts his plan to drive a wedge (pacifier) between us and our pure and simple devotion to Jesus. He tries to offer us the "meat of variety". While we think, we are moving from milk to meat he slowly starves us to death. Diabetes is a disease that creates an inability to use the food we eat. Most of what is eaten is stored as fat, and all along the body starves for the true nutrition it needs. Untreated, the disease can become fatal.

Much of the body of Christ is suffering from a similar disease. We are experts in the things that accompany salvation, feasting until we can hold no more and all the while, we are starving from the lack of salvation **Himself**. Salvation is not the way we act, think, or speak. Salvation is returning to the original purpose for our creation. Salvation means to be made whole. We must remember that God has always intended for us to be his dwelling place. It was the cry of Moses, it was the psalmist's declaration and it is my plea. We must begin to declare our true reason for becoming part of God's salvation. We were chosen by God to carry with us, everywhere we go, the manifested presence of God.

At this point, you might begin to feel confused or angry, maybe even ripped off by your church's *diet* and its leaders. I know I have. After many years of a thematic teaching diet designed to use the scripture to mold God's people into man's interpretation of the "kingdom", I lost my hunger for the Word. I grew tired of unanointed, impassioned men trying to "spoon-feed" me into my *kingdom responsibilities.*

I say unanointed because the anointing breaks the yoke and sets people free. The anointing engenders pure simple devotion to Christ and espouses its recipients into an undying passionate love affair with their Savior and heavenly Father. The anointing is not some mystical, cosmic cloud. It isn't some unique ability granted to only a select few giving them special gifting not available to all of God's children. The Anointing is the blessed third person of the Trinity. The Holy Spirit has come to reveal Jesus and the Father to His children not turn their focus in another direction.

Knowledge, passion and ability can never equal *the Anointing*. These things are of much less importance than our devotion to Jesus and our unconditional **availability**. The Word of God is alive and life-changing if ingested with a sincere desire to know and love Jesus more intimately. No matter what we teach or how "unique" a lifestyle we try to exhibit, it's time we admit it's not producing first century results. Our utter dependency on God, not our formulas, will work.

The hard part is getting through what I call the **denial** stage. I had looked up to the leaders. I didn't want to believe they could have *lost* their anointing. I had even been one of the leaders responsible, in a small way, for the formation of a movement. I had invested many years of my life. Yet the passionate love, peace, joy and *"super-natural"* presence of God I once knew was hard to be found.

It took me many years to admit that we were building beautiful houses, but the manifested presence of God wasn't moving in. Most Church growth in America comes from transfer growth, not new birth. People become unhappy where they're worshipping and try to find the missing "peace" somewhere else. Jesus is what's missing. He said, *"... if I be lifted up I will draw all men unto me."*

I know a man who has a beautiful home, everything I could want! Yet he sits alone almost every evening, separated from his wife and child. The home he built to house a warm and loving family means little to him. In many ways this is a perfect picture of much of the Church in America today.

No matter what kind of war wounds you may have, it is absolutely imperative that you walk in forgiveness. Do not allow unforgiveness to hinder your return to Jesus alone. It is also important to release this anger and frustration to the Lord. I want to encourage you to yell, scream and cry, whatever it takes to get you through the initial stages of denial that the healing may come. Please do not worry about being disloyal. As long as you are seeking to make Jesus your everything, how can you be disloyal? The number of churches in America that are the direct result of a church division is phenomenal.

After I left the movement I had been part of, I felt guilty, almost unclean, as if I could never find God's best again. Subconsciously I was afraid to look God in the eye. Then one day I sat musing about the night I met my Savior, when his love suddenly broke through the doorway of my self-made prison with the key of liberty. It came in the form of a word — **KIDNAPPED!** While I was, still a very young Christian my desire to be and do something great "for God" opened the door for the thief. I was kidnapped by the *things* that accompany salvation. I was held captive by the *"kingdom of god"*.

My *jailers* were shrewd, ruthless, very impersonal and unforgiving. My life of pure love and simple devotion with Jesus had been unknowingly severed. Somehow, after almost 18 years I stumbled out of their clutches. I was hobbling dazed, on the road home. Suddenly I saw my world through God's eyes. As I heard his voice say to me, "you were not disobedient, bad, rebellious, defiled, or disloyal but **kidnapped**" — the cleansing tears began to flow.

I thought of a movie I saw once about a boy who had been kidnapped. Not much of what went on with the boy was revealed, but the torment of the mother and father was clearly seen. Their tireless searching finally yielded the joyful fruit of reunion. As I wept, I sensed I was but one of an endless stream of kidnapped casualties the Father's tireless efforts were recovering.

Our God is a father, not as any father earth has ever known. His capacity for love and affection go so deep, no one could even begin to plumb their depths. Do not make the same mistake Jonathan made. When God removed his anointing from Saul and gave it to David, Jonathan's misplaced loyalty resulted in his death. The *anointing* is everything. It is what our salvation is all about. **THE ANOINTING IS THE VERY LIFE OF JESUS CHRIST!** This life is imparted to us through our union and devotion to Him via the Holy Spirit.

I am not selling division from a church, but a reunion with Christ. My concern is the resulting bitterness that we don't leave at the cross, when the truth of what I am declaring becomes real to you. All God asks in return is pure and simple devotion to him and his Son. What this chapter seeks to do is lift the burden of responsibility that has been placed on the shoulders of God's children by *well-meaning* leaders and/or movements, and encourage us to respond to Jesus Christ's ability again. His ability infuses every fiber of our being with life and sustenance. Our God is a jealous God and the time is coming when he will no longer tolerate a substitute for his salvation. The price he paid for the real thing was too dear. Jesus did it all while he was dying and when it was done he said, *"It is finished!"*

All that remains is for us to remove the pacifier the devil has so skillfully placed in our mouths and open them wide that our God may fill them to overflowing.

"We must pay more careful attention, therefore, to what we have heard, so that we do not drift away. For if the message spoken by angels was binding, and every violation and disobedience received its just punishment, how shall we escape if we ignore such a Great Salvation?"

Kidnapped!